Sunflowers and Seashells

Nature's Miles

John T. Eber, Sr.
MANAGING EDITOR

A publication of

Eber & Wein Publishing

Pennsylvania

Library of Congress
Cataloging in Publication Data

ISBN 978-1-60880-064-3

Proudly manufactured in the United States of America by

Eber & Wein Publishing

Pennsylvania

Foreword

Once again we bring another anthological series of poetry to fruition, and the variety within is sure to engage every reader in some way. In the past twenty-five years, the writing of poetry around the world has changed tremendously. Evolvement in poetic forms, genres, human thought and activity, interpretation, as well as gender, culture, and theory, has provided contemporary writers with the opportunity to create new avenues in poetry, and these volumes reflect such change. Herein, you will see both concrete and abstract poetry, modern and traditional perspectives, metered verse and free verse, confessional and inspirational. Although some are more committed to poetic devices than others, we all seek one common goal—to couple our thoughts, feelings and experiences with the skills we continue hone so that we may share our work with fellow poets. And since many of us have not yet become masters of poetic technique, we find other attributes that can be just as important—personality and expression. T. S. Eliot once wrote, "Poetry is not a turning loose of emotion, but an escape from emotion; it is not the expression of personality, but an escape from personality. But, of course, only those who have personality and emotions know what it means to want to escape from these things." Amateur poets have certainly proven themselves in this respect, as personality and emotion are two key ingredients that weigh heavily in these volumes, drawing empathy from the reader while maintaining a certain level of relatability. I hope your trip through this volume of *Sunflowers and Seashells* is enjoyable and rewarding.

John Eber Sr.

What Good Is Love?

What good is love, ofttimes I wonder,
It should fill you with joy, not tear you asunder.
What does it mean, this soaring emotion,
Can it lighten your woes or insure ones devotion?
If love is so potent, so rich and rewarding,
Please, answer this, is its price worth the courting?

It can't swat a fly or erase a disease,
Lose a beloved—you'll know what loss means...
But love is so different, it can't be defined,
It has many masters, a thousand you'll find.
It wears many faces from gladness to sorrow,
Own it today, it's gone by tomorrow.

Could love be the secret that sweetens our life,
The unspoken words between husband and wife?
Or just sleight-of-hand, the witchcraft we seek,
Does it come out of nowhere to last for a week?
Should you lose all-friends, money and fame,
With or without it, would life be the same?

When all's said and done love is only a word,
To invest it with magic is simply absurd.
Is it nurtured in hell or blest from above,
It begs the question, "What good is love?"
You'll discover the answer once you are bereft,
Assets are worthless, love is all we have left.

Lucille Farrlow
Las Vegas, NV

Love is a powerful emotion. I always felt love could move mountains. The loss of a friend shattered that belief. David and Pam's love was palpable. His work, their daughters, family, and friends were his life. Surely, so much love could conquer any illness. When the inevitable won, I stormed at Fate, demanding an answer to "What good is love?" As strong as it seems, love is only the handle we hang onto until reality sets in. Acceptance comes slowly and it comes hard. So dear caring, doctor, we miss you, we love you, we wish you a gentle, peaceful repose.

Just Getting in Her

Due to the sexual content it might imply,
So reading discretion must be applied,
And your brain won't understand or comply,
Eighteen and under should not even try.

Yonder she stands as plain as can be,
At times she is covered so you can't see,
Seeing her nude is an impossibility,
Just getting in her will be my fantasy.

She doesn't sit high up on a hill,
Touching her copper-tone skin is a chill,
To get to her I might need a pill,
Just getting in her will be my thrill.

From her feet to the top of her head,
She looks like she's all ready for bed,
Like an old maid she can never be wed,
Just getting in her will be my dream instead.

You can't think of her as a movie star,
At her age she's still beautiful by far,
Coming from France she's an ooh-la-la,
Just getting in her can be a rah, rah, rah.

I'd say she has a very quiet personality,
Bringing your imagination back to reality,
When I get there, this will be my plea,
Allow me to go into the Statue of Liberty.

Harry J. Russell
Cheektowaga, NY

I try to put fun into my poetry. "Just Getting in Her" was one of those fun and different poems. When I write like "Just Getting in Her," it becomes one of my better poems. I always liked poetry, ever since junior high. Now I read and write poetry.

Do Not Look Back

One day it will all come to an end

Your collections, treasured or
forgotten, will pass to someone else
Your hopes, plans, and ambitions
will expire

Wins and losses that once
seemed so in particular will fade
So what will matter?
That what you baeegler but
what you gave
That success but significance
That what you learned but
what you taught
Integrity, compassion, courage,
and sacrifice that encouraged
conception and character
will matter.

Jean S. Puckhaber
Ballston Spa, NY

Existentialism at a Rock Concert

I am the chords spilling across these strings
The steady pulse of the drums
The ripple of excitement at song change
I am the rough voice at the mic
The sour fermentation of barley and hops
The tendrils of stale smoke hovering in the air
I am the creak of the stage
The trickles of sweat
The heady feeling in each note
I am the wave of frequencies beating into chests
I am the jumpers
The head-bangers
The screamers
I am the crowd and the band
The ringing of ears
The swaying of bodies
I am their heartbeat
I am the wave they will ride home on
I am this place
And everything wrapped in it
I am the feel of freedom
The sound of release
And the knowledge that we're all here
In this moment
And a part of it

Chivaun T. Perez
Valdosta, GA

Polaroid

Shadows run through the broken walls
From mistakes and memories
As the good life lingers through them all

And as the stars burn down through Heaven's skies
I told you don't waste your breath on those brown-eyed lies

Trails of fiery tears crossed along
And suddenly disappeared like the setting sun

And as the darkness crawled and stole your place
The smoke cleared
And I saw your weathered face

Love died with the rising flames
And shattered down like the pouring rain

And when time stopped
The world became paranoid
And our mistakes and memories
Flashed by like Polaroids

Mackenzie G. Mercurio
Houston, TX

Twenty-First-Century National Anthem

Have you heard how it's done
by the muni-court's judge
in 'is kangaroo kourt?
He's the proof there's no justice!
No conviction for crime!
He's a throwback in time
to the witch-burnin' days
of that place known as Salem!
With the legal aid's help
he's proof justice's dead
as to never have lived . . .
that it's dead as a doornail!
Oh . . . say, have you heard how they get it done in Kansas City . . .
by the muni-court judge,
and 'is kangaroo kourt?!

Denise Marie Bell-Dunson
Kansas City, MO

Everyone Likes Me

"You are what you eat," my father used to say. Well, he was right.
Because in two weeks, I ate forty Snickers bars, and now I snicker.
Once I ate five Caesar salads in one day,
Then starting dating a man name Brutus.
When I ate three bowls of Spanish rice, I became tan.
I tried it again, but it didn't work, so I laid out.
I ate spaghetti for a month straight.
Afterwards, I grew thin like a noodle
And started slipping through cracks and crevices.
I became top-heavy because I ate muffins for year.
I would frequently fall over.
I had a French fry fetish before. I was always greasy,
But could slide in and out of my chair really easily.
Lately, I've been eating a lot of ice cream.
I'm always cold, but everyone likes me.
So it's worth it.

Alexis Black
Chicago, IL

A Beautiful Beginning

I woke up this morning
with the sun shining bright.
I thank God for blessing me
for getting me through the night.

I woke up this morning
with the birds cheerfully
singing, and I knew I was
going to have a beautiful beginning.

I woke up this morning
with a song in my heart,
and I knew God had granted
me a brand-new start.

Susan Bennett
Philadelphia, PA

Sunshine

You are my sunshine on a dreary day
When things seem dark
You lighten the way
When I am sad lost and alone
I think of you and all fears are gone
I thank you for being my friend
If ever you need me I'm here until the end.

Evon White
Lake City, FL

Bravery

Courage is like a light in the darkness,
Willing to stand out while no one else does.
Courage is like a watch,
It ticks and ticks until you find the right time.
Most people don't know they have courage
Until it's too late.
Most people wait and wait
Until all is lost,
And then they feel regret
And feel like they should have let out the animal in them.
A little something called
Courage.

Ryen Rodriguez
Yakima, WA

Untitled

This little life inside of me
Really breaks my heart
Knowing that the time has come
That we will have to part
I'm sorry you won't have the chance
To see your life down here
I'll tell you this, you wouldn't like it
As I shed another tear
I'd bring you up as best I could
If the time was right, I'd keep you
Baby, you know I would
I can't I won't, it's just not right
I think about you always
As I cry every night
When you get up there
You'll look down and see
What life would have been like
Growing up with me
Then you'll realize that I did
What I thought was best
And you'll thank God that I freed you
From this awful mess

Terri Howell
Kingston, NY

Untitled

I've searched the world
o'er
for an antidote
looking like a dope
losing hope
trying . . . trying . . .
hard to cope

Time seems to be
slipping away
from me
as I get older
I know I should be
bolder

Looking up
I see
a glimpse
of light
Where there's light
there's hope
so heart
hold on tightly
to this rope
called life.

Linus Dickson
St. Louis, MO

Linus Dickson was born in St. Louis, Missouri in 1956. He gets his inspiration "sometimes out of the blue" if it's not on subjects of a certain person, place, or event. I have shared my poetry with my high school teacher and students and also with relatives and others. One of my works is forever displayed in photo albums and among the light candles at MCC church as a tribute to those who have lost their life due to HIV/AIDS.

Is Your Life Full?

Is your life full of love?
Do you enjoy what's around you,
Or do you sit and complain
And whine because you are unhappy?
Take a look at yourself in the mirror.
What do you see staring back at you?
A pout, a frown, or a sneer?
Put a smile on your face,
And you will feel much better
When you have a positive attitude.
Focus on the beauty around you,
Have kindness for those you see.
Listen to the lovely music of nature
And of God's lovely, beautiful creatures.
Shut out the evil thoughts,
And focus on the good—
Then your life will be filled
With much joy and excitement.

Tomi Morley Rinard
Kirtland, NM

I am an artist, photographer, and crafter, and love writing poetry; I have since 1950. "Whispering Pines" was my first. I'm inspired by items I see or photos I've taken. The poem "Cool Whip Snow" was written as I had looked out and my trees were covered with this heavy snow, and it reminded me of Cool Whip—mmm, good. I also sing and play piano and organ.

Your Love Is Like a Cup of Tea

Your love is like a cup of tea;
without you, the cup will never be filled.
There may be someone else
who will half-fill it,
but not all the way,
for you are the one who will.

As the day goes by,
your love will grow stronger,
and mine will, too.
Then the cup will be filled,
for our love is like a cup of tea.

While our love grows stronger through the years,
then the cup will overflow,
and our love will be shared the whole life through,
as our love is like a cup of tea.

Theresa Vertrees
Elizabethtown, KY

To a Red-Bellied Woodpecker

Lovely jewel of nature,
You come to my feeder
In your tweed coat
And red cap.
How nice that you dressed for dinner.

Ruth Ann Dean
Lynchburg, VA

Dedicated to My First True Love

After years have passed by
Late nights my heart still cries
Overcoming darkened days with cherished memories we shared
together
My selfishness at fault pushed you away
But with you my heart will forever stay

As my heart cries and my soul dies
Now I know how fragile love is
I wish for one last chance
To tell my first true love

I love you

Andrew Thomas Ferra
Palm Springs, CA

Dear Rain

Dear rain,
I sit in my humble home
and wonder
have we sinned so much
that you are warning us
that it is time to repent?
Are you Heaven's showers cleansing
our souls?
Dear rain,
are you God's way of telling His creations
that they have betrayed
His teachings?
Dear rain,
why do you fall so heavily?
Why do you call upon Poseidon
to flood the towns
and rouse the hurricanes?
Why have you persuaded
Agrestus, Zephyrus, Boreas, and Notus
to escort the chaos you effectuated?
Dear rain,
Why do you take lives,
but then create them?
Dear rain,
I ask you,
why?

Danielle A. Kudlic
Feeding Hills, MA

In a Dream

I sat upon a mountain
With Jesus at my side
He held me gently in His arms
And listened as I cried.

"What is it, child," He asked me
"That has you so upset?"
With heavy heart I struggled
To explain my deep regret.

I searched for words of description,
But ended at a loss
My mind was overcome with memories
Of Jesus on the cross.

For still today we deny Him
With hearts full of lust and greed
In truth, the love of Jesus
Is all we really need.

Patricia M. Boothe
Salem, OH

Newman's Flight

An angel came for me today,
upon a cloud I'd fly away.
On Earth I would be no more,
soon to be at Heaven's door.
Higher and higher I did fly
through the bright blue sky,
and soon I saw fields of green
and ponds of blue;
this is Heaven, I then knew.
Many animals did then appear
to show me around up here.
Then I had to run and play
with all my new friends that day.
I know I will miss you, but I had to go.
They say there is a place up here
where I will wait for you to appear.
The Rainbow Bridge is where I will be,
and someday you will be here with me.

Sandra R. Ignatowski
Lake Forest, IL

Remember

There is but only One God
who loves you more than any other,
whether it be father, son, daughter, or mother.
There is but only One.
He see all that you do and hears
all that you say.
He knows when you rise and when
you rest for the day.
His love is never-ending, and to you
in times of stress
are His angels sent descending to give
you peace and rest,
for you are His special ones,
shining brighter than the sun.
Of all the blessings given unto you,
He asks only one request,
simple as it be—that is to love Him
more and more each and every day
and do your very best.
So remember,
there is but only One true God,
and out of love,
He gave His only begotten Son from above!

Donna Marie
Philadelphia, PA

Otoko no Neko

A lone cat walks the streets, unaware, unknowing.
Where does this graceful being travel to?
Is the path set, or does instinct purely drive him on these roads?
Surely he is looking, searching for one deeply longed for.
A lost child, perhaps a loving family waiting for him,
Or maybe a female captured his eye, rare beauty object of desire.
Maybe he will find her, care for her, raise a family of his own,
Or there is a chance of an unhappy end to this tale.
The truth that no one wishes to know, yet understands all too well,
That even in the kingdom of animals, life can be ripped
From those too young, too soon.
Lovers lost, heroes fallen, families torn apart.
Battles of predator overtaking prey.
Despite these trials of existence, innocence is not yet lost.
Children grow and bloom, the world turns on its invisible axis.
Animals, so like Man, yet a key thing holds them apart.
Is it their beaks, their ears, their tails?
Their talons, their paws, their size, their speech?
No, it is complex, yet simple, this stark epiphany.
Man uses not words, but weapons to cut down their enemy.
Animals fight, but know when to stop,
When to avoid needless bloodshed and who becomes a meal.
Man destroys when scorned, fire raining down from the heavens.
Blind to guilt, pure, foe, friend, male, female, adult, child.
If only Man could learn from the cat as he clearly learned from us.

Sarah E. Milam
Alexandria, VA

To a Daughter/Son

Tough love is the name of the game.
You have brought grief and shame.
Hearts have been cut
While you cut a deal.
You'd lie, you'd cheat, and you'd even steal.

Where have you been
While our hair turned gray?
Were you trapped by the sin that led you away?

There is a key to your heart's bolt.
It will only work from an inside jolt.
The Master of the key awaits.
Are you ready to open the gates?
Your tears can flood away the hate and pain.
Just bow your head in Jesus' name.
Never again will your life be the same!

Peggy G. Marshall
Ararat, VA

Turkey Creek

In the undisturbed quiet there you still are
So peaceful and serene
You evoked nary a ripple when once we stood
Aghast by controversy with big steel
Over your demise
You prevailed and made *Time Magazine*!

Thank you for
Always providing life for the wild
Winding through our seasons establishing
A bond with those who came before and
After us
Your restless springtime too-meandering
'Round, 'neath and o'er stones, rubble
And scree
To rush jubilantly out to Lake Erie
The forever times at your side

Eleanor T. Anthony
Cleveland, OH

Burning Desire

Burning with desire unfulfilled,
I search.
Burning with desire unfulfilled,
I walk.
Burning with desire unfulfilled,
I seek.
Burning with desire unfulfilled,
I wander.
Burning with desire unfulfilled,
I scour.
Burning with desire unfulfilled,
I wend.
Burning with desire unfulfilled,
I stop.
Burning with desire unfulfilled,
I wonder . . .
Will I ever find my burning desire?

Heath E. Hillrichs
Akron, IA

Come Walk with Me

Come walk with me
and hold my hand
the day is cool and bright.
We'll talk of things
from bygone days
shared memories of our life.

Come walk with me
and hold my hand.
We'll smile and laugh
and talk of dreams
for future days.
A new journey has begun.

Wrapped in the warmth of our love
the Earth and its wonders
ours to behold.
We will walk together
hand in hand
through the garden of life,
and along the way, every day,
I'll be loving you.

Edward D. Sanderson
Darien, IL

Fairytale

And like that,
You were gone . . .
And I was left to consider the possibility
That I will never be loved like I wish to be
How strange a feeling
How hopelessly hopeless
The dream of a prince . . . my prince
But the reality is a man . . . just a man
Blinded by your kisses
Lost in your embrace
Deafened by those three words
Where did I go?
How did I lose myself in you?
Jumping in feet first
Eyes shut, heart open
And now . . .
A little more knowledge is in my heart
A little less heart is on my sleeve
I will tell our story at parties and pretend not to care
That once upon a time I kissed a prince
And he turned into a toad.

Crystal Rose McGinnis
Van Nuys, CA

The Surprise Inside

I'm refinishing the dresser passed down from Mom,
Working gently with the inlaid patterns of the wood
That fascinated me when I was young.
(When it's all done, I'm giving it to my son.)
The pace is painfully slow
As the old brownish varnish begins to go,
Shedding layers and layers, and still more layers.
Then, by and by, "It's red!" I cry.
The rich golden-red of the wood is now clear,
I am the first to behold it in many a year!
The naked beauty, its innocence hurts my eyes,
This cedar sunrise, this—what's this—super-surprise?
This newfound glory is glowing a message to me?
Why, yes! (To a poet, everything is therapy!)
I go to the mirror and suddenly I see that,
Through poetry and prayer and painstaking care,
I have slowly been refinishing me.
Shedding layers and layers, and still more layers of
My accumulated goo, my true colors are now clear,
I am the first to behold them in many a year!
The naked beauty, its innocence hurts my eyes,
For I see the child God sees in me—a human sunrise!
The emerging patterns fascinate me as I grow young.
Before I'm all done, I'm giving this to my son.

Carol Priest
Hesperus, CO

Life Becomes the Dream

You are missed dear
Always eager to discuss
Offering your thoughts

Which become the dream
Gathering more ideas
Sharing as we go

Enriching the soul
Laughter and your tender smile
Life becomes the dream

Your smile beckons me
Memories of long ago
You are missed dear

Gallantly you left
On to God's next adventure
Life became the dream

Loretta L. Morgan
Lacey, WA

Our family spirit developed for over a century in pioneer New Mexico, and inspired me to compose poetry to commemorate family members whose stories became an integral part of my childhood dreams and memories. This evolved through Haiku-style poems for each individual, lest we forget their unique spirit and imprint upon our lives. "Life Becomes the Dream" pictures Douglas, my eldest son, who loved all and lived the golden rule. He smiled as his life became the dream, and he departed Earth to enter eternity.

A Book Being Written

A woman appeared before my eyes
Like a book I've longed to read
I know there are some sad chapters
And I know there are wounds that still bleed
But the book is not finished
There are empty pages waiting to be filled
Although many waves have swept over you
One day they will all be stilled
Won't you let me write another chapter
With the greatest Author of all?
Let me write upon your heart
With words and tears that caringly fall
I saw the little girl in you
I saw the radiant woman too
But I am still standing here
Wondering what am I left to do?
I will be a friend to you if you want
And if God's will maybe more
But this can never be
If you stand so far from the open door
And my tears will turn to joy
When your heart is truly made whole
When your joy is made complete
And you dance with your very soul

Jeff A. Knoch
Sacramento, CA

The Broken Tie

Experience can be a friend
Or enemy of heart
Defining who we have become
Defining who we've lost
Two joining lives, I can't forget
A daughter, faith and trust
A father who replaced the first
Who wanted something more
He broke the ties to ease the pain
I let him go
With reaching arms
And doubt.

But now I miss the broken tie
The father who most cared
Through simple words and emails sent
I write my fear to cause him pain
Each word a struggle, holding breath
Afraid he'll fly away
A butterfly upon my hand
A quiver, please don't go!

Valleen C. Mertens
Antioch, TN

Disaster in Haiti

An earthquake with such magnitude wiped out many a Haitian home,
So many disillusioned, still frightened as streets they roam.

Destruction, disaster, and death, finding only despair
To people already impoverished, feeling no one around will care.
Keeping their faith still are Haitians, as many still remain,
Remorse with dying loved ones, so much horror, sadness, and pain.

The cry of despair heard over the world
Was answered by nations with love
To those sorrowing people with prayers to the Creator above.

The golden rule taught us long ago,
In our lifetime, we must answer the call.
To those who are in need today, the world still depends on us all.

Joyce N. Barnum
Richardson, TX

The Strength of a Prayer

I got to ask you this,
What happens if you shoot and miss?
Do you retrieve the shards of your broken arrow
Or do you let your path crumble and narrow?
Do you shoot for the moon,
No matter how much you toil and swoon?
Do you let your eyes glisten over,
And wish for a four-leaf clover?
Because when you just can't stand,
And your life doesn't go as planned,
Your heart wants to scream,
And burn down your dream,
But just remember, God is with you,
And He will give you the strength to get through,
So just pray to Him tonight
And know that it will be all right!

Jennifer M. LaCount
Cincinnati, OH

Barnacles

Howling winds hurled brackish soup,
Battered against the ship's hull.
Fiercely raged the savage storm.
Amidst heaving, angry waves,
Barnacles held their grip still.

Onward through the stormy seas,
Weary sailors manned their posts.
They fought to keep her afloat.
Beneath soggy, laden skies,
Barnacles held their grip still.

Gradually the winds lessened,
The ocean's mighty swells lowered.
Above, heavy skies lightened.
Crewmen drew slow, ragged breath,
Barnacles held their grip still.

Sheree S. Cobbs
Denham Springs, LA

To a Solitary Rose

I knelt closely beside you
As you stood magnificently.
You proved how God can imbue,
Your glory enlivened me.

I thought about bravery
As you glowed in isolation.
You needed no company,
Your thrust declared elation.

I remembered dedication
As you blossomed into God's plan.
You needed no exhortation,
Your devotion crowned your span.

I saw God's benevolence
As you were laid at me feet.
You could not retain radiance,
Your mission was complete.

I bowed my head in gratitude
As you had been a great blessing.
You, dear rose, gave in solitude,
Your praise, I'll keep confessing.

Carrie E. Scott
Lynchburg, VA

God lovingly allows us to enjoy nature and learn from it. So beautiful was a rose that grew on my rosebush in late September that I thought God must have given it all of the beauty of its missing comrades! Then I realized that I should not think about the missing roses because this rose was where it was meant to be and doing what God meant for it to do. It was fearlessly, devotedly, and beautifully carrying out God's plan. Isn't that what we should do in order to live our best lives?

To a Graduating Class Looking Back

As a new year's going through,
we're gettin' a new start,
but from the bottom of my heart,
gonna miss makin' memories when we have to part.
'Cause the rhymes I find are cool
for reminiscing old school.
Reading Harry Potter, trading Pokemon,
goin' from ugly ducklings into beautiful swans.
We've gone through a decade, a century, a millennia,
meshin' with the melodies from Disney's *Fantasia*.
Recession, depression, earthquakes shake my brain,
we'll leave this world better than it was when we came.
Blew through Winnie the Pooh, bird and swine flu,
everywhere in between; *Fresh Prince* and YouTube.
I want to inspire you, admire you,
dedicate a choir to you
for all that you've done
to make my years here such a good run.
We were together from the beginning,
and now it is only fitting
to say a proper goodbye
to break the confines of your minds,
transcend the limits of the times.
My rhymes have rundown the clock, good friends,
and have sadly made this ode come to an end.

Cydney J. Cox
San Antonio, TX

Us

No one knows exactly what happened
We were the fountains meant to fill
Vast voids left by world wars with
No tales told of the strifes ahead
The pain to be paid for pleasures
That talents would be measured not
By our essence but rather by the
Enthrallment of those endeavors
In a world of laissez-faire lessons
Egotistic obsession for possessions
We wonder why with each daybreak
Streets come alive roaring for prey
Troubled we wonder in our escapes
Fault can be fatal 9/11 proved that
We thirst only for more drama
And between the shadows some drain
What if any sentiment remains
For business as usual will reign
Get special interest with permission
To create a new kind of person
On a piece of paper with a pencil
The sellout of another soul a gift
And had we only used common sense
Think where we might be.

Carmen M. Riggs
Kansas City, MO

A Minstrel's Tale

Thousands heard of the kings plan to find the one,
The one artisan with poised, graceful, unyielding hands,
His words so staunch, delivered with such clear demand.
They swept through Maya Land on through to promised band.
Band of artistic types who solely are there to delight
The hearts and minds of the chosen ones in clear sight.
As horsemen gathered with their stock in hand,
Swordsmen's steel glistened free as minstrels sang a symphony.
Warlocks' chants filled the night's air
As if it were to dampen any despair.
For this would be the night, such a magical affair
As the seamstress spins her linens so fair,
A gathering of witches who have come to be seen
On the very same night a young maiden be queened.
No potion, no spell, no ill will to Man
Could spoil the wonderment so carefully planned.
As the potters shine their hardened rock,
Angels swoop down all in a flock.
The maiden be crowned and all were shocked,
They not knew the fair maiden not a little, not a lot.
The young artisan knew all who cast their lot,
And that is the wonderment of it all, is it not?
So go out with your love one quiet night
And rejoice in the glow of celestial light.
You must listen closely, only then you will hear,
Hear the chants and the songs from all the good cheer
For the most artistic one, the dearest artist of the year.

John D. Tassistro
Baton Rouge, LA

In our lives, hopefully someone is there to keep us motivated. My son, Rodney, and my daughter, Angelique, are there for me. Their actions are inspirational, their accomplishments are remarkable. They are my inspiration. Journals for Christmas, notebooks for birthdays; I vow to fill every page, my son. This poem truly came from the promised land of artistic likes for all those who have felt the urgency to act. My heart goes out to you!

Stranded on the Tarmac

Such hate I have never felt
For you
Yes, you . . .
You slithery, long piece of asphalt
Holding me captive nine, ten,
Eleven miserable hours.
Do you want my wallet?
Here, just take my laptop and set me free.
Lord, why did I have to book a seat by the toilet?
The same hate I'm feeling for the
Tarmac . . .
I'm feeling for the toilet.
My own bladder . . . I hate you also.
What do you want from me,
You ugly, tormenting tarmac?
Twelve hours have now passed.
I'm ready to meet my maker.
I submit to you and your piercing runway lights.
I'm melting, melting, melting . . . into the eternal tarmac.

Brian M. Goldspink
Tulsa, OK

Teacher

Dedicated to the non-deservedly creatively oppressed

If you see me
And I am troubled
You could help me
But only hinder me
I could rise above
But left stuck in the quagmire
Being filled with prejudice
I do not accept your empty threat
I move for a repeal
My talent and dedication
Combined with my faith and resolve
Will be decisive and prevalent
And leave your peers appalled
At you

Matthew Phillips
Bay City, MI

Ode to My Child

Are you the child I pray to God for
from jump whom I adored—now the city whore?
Are you my beloved I made a pact with
prayed against the devil's sift, now bereft and so adrift?

Now you are lost, but I was so attentive
You were so full of promise, grasping all God's incentive
Led astray, forsaking purpose and plan,
head squarely stuck in proverbial sand

The Word of God is true, His promise everlasting
Repent and get it right with fervent prayer and fasting
Are you the son, a great man from the womb?
Am I to assume you are short for the tomb?

You take it in stride, never missing a beat
You can run but cannot hide, can't you feel the heat?

I still have hope, a river, in fact
God still floats my boat whatever I may lack

So loving so kind, I believe, still held in His fist
He and I together, betrayed by a kiss.

Annie A. Hines
Tacoma, WA

Pledge of Allegiance

I pledge allegiance
to the flag of my country,
the home of the saved and the free,
and to the King of salvation
who gave His life for me.

I pledge allegiance
to the flag of my country,
the home of the brave and the free,
for many have died that I might live
in a land where there's liberty.

I pledge allegiance
to the flag of my country
and to the republic for which it stands,
one nation indivisible
under God's almighty hand.

Rosemary Frick
Roy, WA

Time

Time is something we cannot comprehend
For it never had a true beginning
And is something that will not ever end
Time will soar on like a bald eagle's wing
Time can be compared to the bright blue sky
The blue sky seems to go on forever
Time lasts too, so it never says goodbye
For He who made time is very clever
And though we must stay within time's limits
God is not affected by time itself
Sometimes time seems to move like fast comets
And time is hard to understand yourself
Though only in Heaven we understand
We will still ponder in this earthly land

Brianna M. Battle
Wellington, FL

I'm thirteen years old and I live in Wellington, FL. I love writing poems and stories. I also own and ride horses and I love to draw. I'm in seventh grade, and the reason I wrote this poem is actually because it was an English assignment that we had to write a sonnet. The reason I chose the subject of time is because it seemed like a challenging subject, and I prefer a challenge. It is also a subject that has always annoyed me because it's so incomprehensible.

Here I Stand

Lovely and unwounded
A heart wide as the sea
Did you comfort me?
How great was my pain?

Deep in my heart,
Tears overflow the walls
Day 'n' night and night 'n' day,
Destroyed without mercy.

No . . . healed from disaster.
Deep within my soul
I was reminded of what fills me with hope,
Peace, and brings me happiness.
Yes . . . I am complete.

Catrina K. Maycock
Buena Park, CA

One More Night of Bliss

Oh, life, from you, I ask only this;
Let me have soon, one more night of bliss!
Or let it be day! But please let it be!
It's all that I dream of, oh, grant this to me!
Give me three wishes, I ask only this;
Let me have soon, one more night of bliss!
Ecstasy lies there, just out of our sight,
Then how did we find it that one lovely night?
Let me fall in those feathers just once more,
Open for me that inaccessible door!
Let me roll in the clouds and walk in the fire.

Show me the way, for I burn with desire!
If I cannot have this, how can it be
That you were so cruel as to show this to me?
Some people live and never know it at all.
I know it, I felt it, please let me fall!
Let me fall off the world and lay on a star,
Let me enter that void, no matter how far.
I love life. I love you. I ask only this;
Let me have soon, one more night of bliss.
I love you, I need you all these long years
In sadness, in passion, in laughter, in tears.
I love you so much, I ask only this;
Let me have soon, one more night of bliss!

Marilyn Smith Fifer
Midlothian, IL

Standing Proud to Be an American

Did you see my mom in the war?
She was a member of that brave military force
She was the one with her finger on the trigger
She was the one in the front seat of the chopper
She was the one in the camouflage wardrobe
With dust in her hair and sand in her teeth
Standing proud to be an American

Did you see my mom in the war?
She was the one on that big old ship
Well-trained and bent on doing her job 110 percent
Pushing a pulley or loading a missile
Following in the footprints of those before her
Blazing a trail for those who follow her
Standing proud to be an American

Did you see my mom in the war?
When it is all over and won
She is the one with the soft touch in the pretty dress
Fragranced with the sweet smell of success
And when I hear that she is coming home
I am the one with all love in my heart
A smile on my face and kisses to share
Standing proud to be an American

Janice A. Caracter
Hampton, VA

Love Is Patient

I gaze upon you from afar;
Your eyes are lit like shining stars.
Your lips become my source of life,
I want to kiss them day and night.

But you do not know how I feel about you
Because I'm too shy to tell you, it's true.
So until that day, my sweet, sweet crush,
When we joke around, I'll continue to blush.

I have a blast when I'm with you,
Not a care in the world, no feeling blue.
You light up my life every day and night.
I wish I could tell you, but I'm afraid you might
Run away like a galloping deer
Who sees the hunter that's coming near.

And so I hope, one day, my sweet
You will come to me and our lips will meet.
You will tell me that you have feelings for me, too.
We will have so much love that we'll both be consumed.
We will bask in the glow of it day and night,
For our love will continue with no end in sight!

Jason E. Hendela
E. Haven, CT

Snow Falling Like Commas

Snow falling like commas
On a blank page
Dividing rocks and trees from poles
Deleting nature's errors
To begin a new document
Filled with hushed excitement

Footprints deeply embedded like words
Creating fresh paths from old tales
A search for food, a phrase
Then pursuit and capture
Coyotes howling success
Like writers
Hawking bestsellers

Carol Strazer
Red Feather Lakes, CO

You may wonder why I chose snow for my poem's subject. This spring, we've had many snowstorms, and our community's lake is still frozen. Even though it's mid-May, my neighbors shovel and grumble about the snowy slush. The white aspen trees stand leafless. Near the mail shed, a shaggy moose chews on snow-encrusted willows, and two tiny hummingbirds shiver on my feeder. In the northern Colorado Rockies at 8,700 feet, winter is long—spring is short, yet I love the snow, our small log cabin, and my family even more.

truly free verse

teaching freshman comp courses
be damned

the immaculate logic of grammar
and syntax
has annihilated the illogic
of my poetry
forced the fine insanity
of my verse
into prosaic idiocy

i hereby sentence clumsy clauses
to an elegiac death
banish paragraphs and parts of speech
to lyrical limbo
consign commas and semicolons
to purgatory
and condemn all unlovely things of even
line length
to milton's fiery inferno

may perdition take them every one

Joseph H. Kempf
Indianapolis, IN

Groundhog Day

I sit and reflect
running through everything I encountered
everything that greeted me
after my ascent from solitude and faced
the sunlight
Absentmindedly I stared back
every look I received
only heard everything within earshot
I didn't stop to actually take the time
to comprehend until now
As I recline and I finally catch up
with my thoughts
analyzing mistakes made
pondering what I should have done
only to never regain the chance to do it right
Scenarios play endlessly taking a break from reality
telling me what my life could be like if I let it be
My mind pleas with me incessantly—do that!
Be that! You are that! Now just be it!
But I silence the plea and drift off to sleep
to prepare for the same journey tomorrow

Cotrell A. Loftin
Garfield Heights, OH

What Fall Brings

Most of all the birds have gone,
The blue jays are still hanging on.
The mornings are crisp,
The afternoon, you burn a little bit.

The morning has fog.
The sun burns hard and long.
It looks so warm outside.
When opening the door, you want to go hide.

We changed back the time.
Extra hour of sleep, it's about time.
It gets light earlier,
Also gets dark earlier.

The squirrels are gathering their nuts.
The buck deer is getting ready to rut.
The hunters are using the bows and arrows.
When they take their aim, it better be straight and narrow.

Shirley A. Nestor
Parsons, WV

Python

Old Silas Rand, they can't catch him.
No use trying, they never can.
Why? It's his home turf.
As a kid, he knew the 'Glades
Like the back of his hand.
Oh, those islands of grass,
Where slithers wide and slithers long
A new kid on the block fears neither gator nor Man.
Python!
Too much whiskey, a barroom fight gotten out of hand
Had Silas leaving a man dying, a knife in his chest
On the streets of old Deland.
By the crack of dawn, Silas was 'Glades-bound.
Every island of grass he knew so well.
Hiding with the gators, he'd not be found.
No lawman would wade through those sewers of hell.
We figured old Silas made well his escape.
Alas, late in September, his family gave up all hope
When the law told them by an island of grass
Filled with water, they found his boat.
Poor old Silas, must've been quite a shock.
In those islands of grass,
There's a new kid on the block,
Slithering wide and slithering long.
Fears not a gator and certainly not a man.
Python!

David Avard Illsley
Edgewater, FL

First Kiss

It was as fleeting as a lightning bug's glow on a dark night
A tiny pulse of light that startles you as its beauty blinds your heart
traps your might
So poignant and precise that nothing so pure had I played a part
It was a kiss not mine for the taking the giving of it stilled my heart
A gift given so freely to remain unopened till now my heart grown up
with time
I had never imagined an act with such purity could or would ever be mine
Someone so young with so much depth could see me and want to taste
That anyone so young would want to give something as fatal and final
without haste
My first kiss

The softness and thoughtfulness of his lips still touches my soul's lore
Tasting of sunshine and spun candy with the firmness of a young man's core
I remember a fluttering sound in my imagination it had to be angel wings
Lashes longer than my own liken to a soft breeze against my face my
soul now sings
The magic of the moment would become my compass with life-altering force
He fearless and beautiful with the kindest eyes that changed my heart's course
I now remember relive and unwrap this tender fragile gift from above
It being the moment in time where you know you'll be able to give and
receive love
One kiss at a time

Kay Jo Collins-Anderson
Modesto, CA

I had a childhood filled with tragic deeds, but there was magic, too. It was my mother's love. I only recently found it gives me great joy, and the magic now comes from my children's love. I am truly blessed and use words to bring light to the dark memories. A beautiful boy gave me a gift. This is my way of giving one back. I feel deeply honored that anyone would read my poems and I hope it takes you to a beautiful place. I wish you all God's grace.

My Sweet Rose

This rose is just a symbol
Of my ever-growing love.
Its petals, leaves, and fragrance
Get their life from God above.

This love that grows within my heart
Grows stronger every day.
Unlike this rose, it will not die,
Our love is here to stay!

The sweet aroma of your love
That blossoms in my heart
Sustains me daily through the times
When we must be apart.

So as you look upon this rose
And smell its sweet perfume,
Imagine you are in my arms
In the privacy of your room.

Remember, "What you think about
You bring about" . . . it's true.
So keep me present in your mind,
And I will be with you!

Phillip A. Colombo
Doylestown, PA

The Locust Chorus

The locust chorus louder sings,
  With thrumming drums to Heaven flings
The grand finale, summer's end,
  With autumn just around the bend.
As temperatures still higher soar,
  That buzz crescendos to a roar
That fills my soul, rings my ears,
  As dog days' chorus final cheers
Now bid the summer to delay
  And linger on for one more day.
But summer's heat is nearly o'er,
  And temperatures will soon slip lower
To cool the eve, then it's not long
  Till chill will still the locusts' song.
Embrace this music of the Earth,
  The seasons end to bring new birth,
And thus, renewal comes to all,
  Through summer, winter, spring and fall.
Our fall and winter fade and then
  Our spring reawakes, without, within.
As seasons into seasons blend,
  We see, in truth, no song will end.

Pat S. Buhl
Tulsa, OK

Music on the Prairie

The beautiful music of the symphony,
  in these surroundings, seemed as if
  Mozart were performing a piano concert
  in the midst of the prairie.

Men and women, in their own little corner
  of the outdoor Osage Hills,
  listening, feeling the strong rhythm
  of the brass and woodwinds,
  with intriguing sounds of the violins
  playing on one's heart strings.

Blankets spread, crumbles left
  from a picnic lunch—spilled cola, ants.
The fresh air smelled of new mown hay on the meadow,
  leaves rustling on the trees,
  then the slur of the piccolo returned to the
  melodic, harmonic music of the orchestra.

Listening to the soloist play the flute
  on indented keys for her fingers,
  trilling, holding for a moment,
  the chirping like sound of a bird,
  as if singing, frolicking about in the air.

The virtuoso of the musicians,
Saint-Saens' "Carnival of the Animals;"
  ah, sweet music on the prairie.

Marilyn G. Fitzpatrick
Pawnee, OK

2008 NCAA Tournament

Bounce, dribble, pass, shoot
Red, white, and blue uniforms
At halftime, Kansas 33, Memphis 28
Memphis ties the score and gets ahead
5:10 left in game, KU down by six
2:12 left in game, KU is nine points behind, 51-60
1:23, Dorsey fouls out
Chalmers shoots free throws
KU scores
Collins gives ball to Chalmers
Chalmers shoots, 3.9 seconds remaining
Memphis hits three-pointer and nothing but net
Ties game 63-63
Overtime
Memphis gets tipoff
KU scores 12 points
Memphis scores 5 points
Jayhawks are champions 75-68
We got nothing but net and a national title
History repeats itself
"Rock, Chalk, Jayhawk"
Bounce, dribble, pass, shoot

Lisa A. Ball
Welda, KS

Tiger Ray's Victory for Life

Howdy neighbors, howdy,
Why don't you come on in?
I'll tell you 'bout my Tiger,
The very best of friends.
I'll tell you 'bout my Tiger,
The love he showed to me—
How he put his paw 'round my neck
As cute as sweet as can be.

We have baseball in the springtime,
We have football in the fall.
If you don't have your Tiger,
Then you have no fun at all.
I had a talk with Tiger,
I shouted and he purred.
He showed me love and kindness,
Hallelujah was his word.

Do you want to meet your Tiger?
I'll tell you what to do.
Just reach out and love someone,
And you'll get your Tiger, too.
Get along with your Tiger,
Get along with Tiger Ray.
You ought to see my Tiger—
He's the king of cats, I say.

Stephen R. Williams
Tulsa, OK

Tiger Ray was not just a lively, energetic, natural hunter, but also a very loving cat. Tiger Ray was very uplifting and encouraging. A lot of songs, poems, etc. talk about negative, bad, gloomy, and sad things, and the main theme of "Tiger Ray's Victory for Life" is about love and encouragement. This little poem just barely scratches the surface of the love Tiger Ray showed. So just sit back, read, and use your imagination with this little poem, and you will love it.

Benediction for a Millennium

May sun by day
and moon by night
illume the path,
a guiding light
to lead us safely on our way
beyond misfortune's
reach and wrath,
in refuge far
or solace near,
away from illness, hunger, fear.
Tolerance learn,
compassion feel,
whereby
preserve humanity . . .
division to union,
universal communion,
most blessed be.

Esperanza Guerrero
Pasadena, CA

As a child of the Mohave Desert, raised in Needles, CA, oral tradition and storytelling was an integral aspect of both my parents' families. My concept of the written form is that of extension or extrapolation of the oral form. My poetry is specifically intended to be spoken aloud. This particular piece aspires to offering a bit of hope as the new millennium unfolds and progresses.

The Earth

God made humans in charge of planet Earth
Where all provisions for our lives abound
Replete with vital knowledge since our birth.
Should we not life's gifts profound?
Indeed, how marvelous all seasons bring!
How dreary 'tis in autumn when leaves fall
But then fresh, cute ones will put forth in spring.
Come winter icicles bedeck trees tall.
For awesome, diverse gifts, hear the bells chime
Thanksgiving tunes, for golden grains abound
For the frolicking birds in summertime.
Cheer up! There's festivity all around!
As stewards, we must clean this sphere with mirth
Which is our home, the gorgeous planet Earth.

Ligaya V. Yuzon
Alameda, CA

In One Hour

It's all over! Just think—no time left to change your mind.
You waited too long! You thought you had lots of time to do things
your way. You were wrong. You heard the truth, but refused it.
Now the ones who told you are all gone.
In one hour, the system changed.

The warning came. You scoffed and laughed.
You thought you knew it all!
Pride came first, followed by greed.
Evil crept in—and then the fall.
You didn't check the source. No more time for you to heed the call.
In one hour, the world changed!

The price was paid; you thought it foolish—the message of the cross!
You had your chance, but refused, and now you're left with dross.
Weeping and wailing and wishing—the truth you had not lost.
In one hour, your thoughts changed!

"Oh, if only I had read the Book!" The message was plain to see,
For God so loved the world that He gave His only Son for you and me.
He took our sins upon Him and shed His blood upon a tree.
In one hour, our fate was changed!

For those who still have time to choose, make your choices right.
Read the Book, accept His love, He will change your plight,
For the day of the Lord comes as a thief in the night!
In His power, you'll be unchained!

Be ready when He comes; prepare to meet Him in the air!
In the twinkling of an eye, you'll meet your Savior there.
You'll be among the wheat and not the tare.
In His power, you'll be changed!

Kathleen A. Belcher
Dallas, TX

I was inspired to write this poem while reading the Book of Revelation, Chapter 18, verses 10, 17, and 19 referring to the things that will happen "In One Hour."

A Trilogy of One

Bleary images float the clouded sky. . . .
I was a child of many dreams.
Remembering, standing on my father's boots,
Looking up to him, a little half above
His breeches-covered knees, picked me up
And brushed his bearded face against my cheeks,
Then let me go. . . .

My mother and I knelt in prayer each evening glow,
Kept ears keen for returning footsteps that we always knew.
Even his pet by the garden gate lay sullen in wait
Till Mother's knees turned stiff and lips in prayers ceased.

Now, no longer a child of many dreams,
My man stood tall, well-trimmed like the picture
In the frame; before him looking up, three tykes adoring,
Scooped them in his grasp,
Buried his face on them and left. . . .

The scene has faded like a dream and the boys
Have grown rugged and brawn, well-bred in any span,
Picked up where father left—one to Afghanistan,
Another to Fallujah, the last stayed for Mother America.
And here I am, unlike my mother, with tears no more,
Finding solace in waiting.

Adoration P. Victorino
Los Angeles, CA

I always have a soft spot in my heart for the mothers and wives of soldiers around the world. They are the unsung heroines behind their men while fighting for peace and freedom. While being left behind, the anguish is compounded, especially with very young children. I know because my husband was a World War II veteran, a prisoner of war, and a recipient of a Bronze Star Medal for Valor in the Korean War. This poem is a tribute to the women of fortitude. May they be strengthened in their faith and devotion as partners to a worthy cause.

Pruning Azaleas in Spring

A quiet morn in early spring,
My sun-starved soul, awakening
From winter's dark and dreary days,
Decides to bask in Heaven's rays.
With pruning shears, I make my path
Toward the azalea bush out back.
I start the trimming at the top.
But when I reach the side, I stop
To give the baby black snake there
A chance to find another lair.
The bees are busy 'round the blooms,
Though many petals meet their doom.
The branch will grow back, strong and true
With blossoms of impressive hue.
I think of other things I know
That need a pruning, so to grow.
And suddenly, it's all quite clear
That pruning plants from year to year
Is like the care we each must take
Within our lives if we're going to make
A healthy, thriving go of it
While here on Earth to keep us fit.
For pruning jealousy and hate,
Forgiving wrongs, soon and late,
Will make us strong and set us free
To be all we were meant to be.

Margaret R. Green
Nokomis, FL

Feelings

Sometimes I just don't understand
Why these days are so tough.
As if my life hasn't been rough enough.
Having to live each and every day
Not ever knowing if these feelings will ever go away.
All there is left for me to do is
Pray and pray each and every day.
A hope that these feelings will
Soon somehow, someday, just please go away.

Kali A. Hovestreydt
Sunland, CA

A Friend

A friend is
A push
When you've stopped
A word
When you're lonely
A guide
When you're searching
A smile
When you're sad
A song
When you're glad

Patrice Kasper
Carol Stream, IL

Everybody Loves My Mother

Everybody loves my mother,
From her "one size fits all" hugs
To her fragrant smell of lilies.

Everybody loves my mother,
Her heart would swallow you.
From her giving hands
To hold you tight,
Morning, noon, or night!

Everybody loves my mother,
Her face all aglow,
Her smile would light many candles
As her warmth lit your heart,
Sparkles flare when her presence is near.

Everybody loves my mother,
Love to surround you, warmth to warm you,
Hands to hold you until all are beheld with love.

Everybody loves my mother,
And you know why?
God made her a mother,
A virtuous wife,
Tiny tot, granny, sister, daughter, friend, and Cubbie.
I call her my Motherdear,
My garden of care, planted with love!

Khoda L. Stone
Louisville, KY

Hero

He will never know me personally.
  Never see my dripping eyes.
My prayers of thanks through whispered tears,
  he will not hear.

The thrill I feel at the sound of
  a bluebird's call during a picnic in summer,
my heart remembers his blood
  bought me the right to enjoy.

The voice of his sacrifice sings to me
  from every hill.
Each wave of the flag fills me with pride
  for his valor and honor.

No one asked him.
  No one forced him.
He gave his all, and more
  for his fellow countrymen.

May God in Heaven
  send every blessing
to the brave one we call
  American veteran.

Erin E. Robinett
Portland, OR

I am fifty-three years young and the fifth of nine children. Mom taught us all to read before kindergarten. My family has always encouraged my writing. I wrote "Hero" in honor of my eldest brother, John. Although it is composed in the male gender, I dedicate it to all servicepersons. My brother is a Vietnam veteran and I wrote this poem for him because I wanted him to know I understand what war costs. I love him very much and am so proud to be the sister of an American veteran.

Man's Ruining It All

Radiant sunbeams streaming down,
Shining through pines, striking the ground.
  Whispering sounds through tops of the trees
As they sway to and fro from the gentle breeze.
  Walking the path that winds through the wood,
I'd live in this place, if only I could.
  Rabbits and squirrels scamper and play,
A fawn looks up, then darts away.
  Small, bubbling stream, water ice cold,
Beautiful place, as precious as gold.

  Man-made machines cutting trees down,
Thundering sounds as they hit the ground.
  Whispering sounds gone with the trees,
Wind blows strong, no more gentle breeze.
  Path is gone now, can't walk through the wood,
I'd put it all back, if only I could.
  Rabbits and squirrels have no place to play,
No more fawns, they've all gone away.
  The smell of fresh pine is gone from the air,
They're destroying everything that God placed there.
  The stream is gone with its water ice cold,
Man's ruining it all for a handful of gold.

Marlene J. Campbell
Cameron, MO

Writing poetry since 1963, most avidly in 1995-97. Distinguished member of and published with National and International Poets Societies, Famous Poets, and Sparrowgrass. Fifteen Editor's Choice Awards. Attended the 1995 International Poetry Convention in Washington, DC. Placed in the International Poetry Hall of Fame on the Web and *Who's Who in Poetry*. Over 400 poems written on various subjects. *Poetry by MJC—Expressing Me* copyright. 1995-97, read numerous poems over local radio and published in the local newspaper. Self-published three booklets. Three children and four grandchildren. Moved from Pennsylvania to Missouri in 1975. Grandmother taught me to look for beauty in everything and late husband encouraged me.

Untitled

Do you really think you can prepare yourself
For the time when tragedy comes?
Do you know just how you'll act and feel
When it comes to your own loved ones?
You always expect the old to go first,
Which is really the way it should be.
The young and the strong and the healthy should live
For many years, don't you agree?
Why should their young life be cut off so soon,
Their fun years were all too few.
There should have been many more years for them.
They had so much living to do.
You look at their pictures, you just can't believe
That they're not just away for the day.
You cry until the tears won't come,
Your grief is here to stay.
There seems to be a void so big
That nothing can fill
Until the time comes to cross over that void
As sooner or later you will.
You'll greet the ones you love so much,
You'll have so much to say,
And be so happy and content
That you are here to stay.

Rene E. Bingham
Cap May, NJ

The Youths of Today

How happy are they, the youths of today,
as they grovel and struggle on life's blithesome way?
How sadly and fleetly they ensnared
as they run through life's courses like they never cared!

Often one wonders how deeply they think
as they follow in the footprints of the masses which sink.
Proudly and vainly run they to the brink,
stopping occasionally to converse with a shrink.
Now in this corner, then over yonder,
but for the most part, ending nowhere but under.

To mitigate or end this unhealthy trend,
I hereby strongly recommend
that you be constantly on guard
against all that is bad and appears to be hard.

Immerse yourselves on all occasions,
whether you be working or playing,
doing things that are uplifting.
With eyes always open and your minds alert,
surmounting all impediments and excruciating incidents.

Be patient and plodding, forever enduring the storms and the stresses
which create your distresses!
Be kind and progressive, hardworking and loving
to keep on resolving your trials unending
because they will keep on returning
till your living has ended!

John F. Redhead
Brooklyn, NY

I Love to Celebrate Christmas

I love to celebrate Christmas
And here's the reason why
It started God's plan for salvation
When He sent His Son to die

I love to celebrate Christmas
With the shepherds and kings that were wise
I wonder if Mary and Joseph
Knew their baby was born to rise

I love to celebrate Christmas
And listen for the angels to sing
Glory to God in the highest
To the newborn baby King

I love to celebrate Christmas
My King was born in a manger
His only crown was a crown of thorns
I can't think of anything stranger

I love to celebrate Christmas
Thanking the Father above
For sending His Son Jesus
And starting Christmas love

Valanna M. McCurry
Fruitland Park, FL

A Stone

I had in mind to plant a garden
So I began the clearing of a space.
I was about to toss away a stone,
But felt it fit so well within my hand.
On close inspection, I traced a thread of magma
That, in eons long ago, had solidified
Within this glinting, mica-speckled stone.
Born from the fierce heat, roiling deep
Within Earth's bosom and bound in the choking grip
Of the mighty denseness,
The molded stone emerged from that awful cauldron
To then endure the persistent grinding
And the jarring by the thrashing elements.
The stone was gnawed upon like a bone,
Rolled from place to place, buried,
Then exposed again to be pounded more.
Now worn smooth, which seemed to have a softness,
The stone had a soothing, a triumphal feel within my hands.
I then surmised this stone was as though a flower
And I kept it in my garden.

Carmen M. Ruestow
Boulder, CO

Pianist

Eighty-eight keys,
each with a note assigned,
played with ease
by the hands of mankind.

Smooth layers
filled with pure black and white,
owned by the player's
musical flight.

A sound so intense,
and a picture played so clear.
A story filled with suspense
until the end is near.

The notes fly out
through the tips of one's fingers,
no room for doubt
while the last note lingers.

The final demise
sails through the air
as the player's hands rise
and leave the keyboard bare.

Lauren N. Matthews
Honey Brook, PA

A Colorado Morning

There's nothing prettier than a Colorado morning

The air is so clear
As time stands still
Dirt roads with dust settling

Being fifteen
Not knowing what life would bring

What promises in sunrise lie
Only knowing and enjoying the morning
As time stands still
As if in a photo frame

Magnificent mountains to the west
Prairies never ending to the east
Standing barefoot on a cool cement porch
On a Colorado morning

What fates are whispered in the wind
Not for us to know just now
But to ponder just the same—on a Colorado morning

Marcy L. Bowser
Newark, OH

Reflections

Life is strife, confusion king
Perplexing young and old.
The secret which protects us
True creations from the mold.

The cycle clear, begins and ends
With a focal point supreme,
Acceptance of a distant ghost
Divides frivolity.

Try to tell the lesser-aged
Of knowledge yet unlearned.
The fight will be a battle lost
Well-conceived, yet undiscerned.

Rolling sand maintains its shape,
Endures the pounding rain.
Throughout the land, young lions roar
And strut their regal manes.

Reflections of infinity
Define one's self-esteem.
Observe the hourglass ticking,
The fundamental dream.

Michael E. Webb
Circleville, OH

New Dawn

Life on a farm enhanced my childhood,
Nurtured by nature and wonder.
Each sleepy dawn slipped through the sunrise
And scattered sunlight asunder.

The old grandfather clock chimed the hour,
Trees stretched their arms, stirring a breeze.
Songbirds sang sweet music of splendor,
Waking the butterflies and bees.

Bugle Boy, the rooster, cocked his head,
Crowed "Reveille," his charming call.
Chickens began chattering for corn,
Cows mooed in rhythm from each stall.

Daylilies strutted their fancy hues,
Honeysuckle scents swept the air,
Morning glory vines glistened with dew,
One more new dawn to dream and dare.

Today, I wake to an alarm clock
With the din of cars driving by,
And cherish my homemade childhood days
As a new dawn swells through the sky.

June E. Nash
Morton, MS

The Run

Who's running?
Why do they run?
These people run for office.
They run to give service.

Though they are willing to serve,
The price they pay is dear,
Yet they run like a deer
Who is ever so dear,
Who's constantly alert.
Why do they run?

Who is running?
People who want to take charge.
There's so much to be done.
Why do they run?

The years in the office,
This brings wear and tear,
Yet they must run,
So when they finish,
The running is almost over.

Rosie M. Clark-Sims
Arlington, TX

I started writing poetry at an early age. In the school I attended, the teacher instructed her class in writing a variety of poems. I began to write poetry that expressed my observations of life. I was reared in Waco, TX, and graduated from Paul Quinn College. I also attended East Texas State University. I've taught at several schools in the Dallas area. I have always enjoyed reading, writing, and listening to music.

Dance

She dances in the verdant wood waiting for her consort
Long tresses gleam with Titian flames
Spiral curls pirouetting in sunlight
Crimson lips hint at the flush of her mood
Seductive curves reveal a bounty in her breasts
Singing in the summer heat, ready to embrace her lover
Her dance is the heartbeat of the Earth.

He runs in the viridian forest, eager for his inamorata
Raven locks glint aubergine under a dappled sun
Scarlet lips whisper virility on the wind
A crown of horn speaks of his potency
His wild, vernal zeal turns toward efflorescing days
An urgent hunger for her kiss brings him to her
Yearning for release in his dance.

Beltane revelers frolic, weaving inward, outward
Ribbons of vermilion and alabaster undulate with life
Splashes of pine, sage and vivid green flash by
Trees bear witness to the magic of their dance
Everywhere, creation bursts forth,
A kaleidoscope of possibility in bloom
Lucid passion and euphoria are within the grove
As goddess and god sing, life becomes the dance.

Lana M. Barry
Portland, OR

Trouble in the Church

Turmoil reigned in the church.
Members were so few.
God blessed both,
but old ways clashed with new.

As ledgers emerged red,
the ministries worried.
Recession called
for docket oppression.

Satan played his game.
In working well,
everyone should've quelled
wanting their way.

Instead of prayer,
bickering prevailed,
people bailed,
taking money with them.

When flocks thinned
and programs got sparse,
ministries feared
which souls they missed.

Kim A. Taylor
Wichita Falls, TX

Love—What Is Love?

What is love? Love is a laughing child
Love is watching a child learn to walk
Love is sharing gifts with family and friends
Love is fighting for freedom of one's country
Love is a newborn baby
Love is the exchanging of vows between husband and wife
Love is showing a child how to read and write
Love is caring for the homeless and giving shelter
Love is giving a coat to someone shivering in the cold
Love is Jesus Christ giving Himself for our sins
Love is life given to us by God Himself
Love is forgiving those who had wronged another
Love is feeding the hungry
Love is going without to care for others
Love is sharing justice for the wrongly accused
Love is giving oneself to help another
Love is building a home for a homeless family
Love is caring for a dying person
Love is taking care of an injured animal or bird
Love is beautiful
Love is mighty
Love is giving
Love is giving a lift to someone who needs it
Love is taking care of a sick child
Love is a mystery
Love can hurt
Love is God our heavenly Father

Sharon Jean Duschell
Kansas City, MO

I have always loved poetry. Poetry to me is quiet music and telling a story, whether it's unrequited love, something animals have done as pets or in nature, personal relationships with people, or even the love of God. I lost many people in my fifty-seven years, but my love for God has never faltered. I also had cancer; I'm coming up on six years of being cancer-free and cured. I love animals, and I love to watch them at play. I love doing puzzles and games. I love collecting unicorns, dragons, angels, stuffed toys, holiday jewelry, clothes, etc.

Who Am I?

Who am I—I who can fly,
soar high above mountain peaks,
spin and carry the wind, and then
touch the tops of fields of green,
tilt the Earth serene?

In an instant, my presence is as pure
as gold, as majestic as the sun,
I'm told.

Who am I—I who can soar,
and touch the ocean shores, then
change seasons for all to see?

Who am I—in all my forms,
I am goodness, peace, serenity.

Denise B. Waller
Gladys, VA

Inside Out and Outside In

Inside out and outside in
Where, oh, where do I begin?
If I was inside out or outside in,
How would I look? Fat or thin?
My poor tongue would be hanging out.
My eyes could not see.
They'd be backwards, inside of me.
My nose would be outside in,
I'd look so comical, just couldn't win.
My stomach would be falling low.
This is not the way to go!
My lungs would make me cough and choke,
This, you see, is not a joke!
My bones would be shiny and white.
You'd see them in the darkness of the night.
Oh, goodness, what a mess I'd be.
Inside out or outside in
Is not the way for you or me!

Irene Mernagh
Phoenix, AZ

Shar-Pei Silk

A Shar-Pei is a wrinkled silk shirt
Sprawled on the carpet
the sleepy chemise yawns
as more wrinkles become apparent
Black buttons gaze aimlessly
awaiting sounds in the vicinity
Waist and neck wrapped in wrinkles
embellished on black material
Massive folds consume and cover the tail
especially when waving in the wind
Creases centered on elbows and arms
as clumsy movements multiply
The silky Shar-Pei is a fragile fabric
and must be handled delicately
While the wrinkled shirt should be ironed
a Shar-Pei must never be ironed
One can pet the furry fabric
and wrinkles will momentarily
disappear

Julie A. Garton
North Glenn, CO

retrospect

who are you
what comes to mind
you may know what i am talking about
when there is nothing here to find
or do you think that all you are
is memories about the past
some sort of egoic mental structures
that you may think will last
who and what are you really are in essence
the mind can never know
for it is ever seeking, always wanting
something it can't find
which is a way to define the present moment
by looking back in time
who are you
now what comes to mind
beyond the questions and answers
beyond the thinking mind
beyond duality and definitions
beyond space and time
who you are is everything
and nothing that you can seek and find
you can only be the oneness
from a cosmic frame of mind

Patrick J. Wong
Tehachapi, CA

Shades of Hue

Living is green
Loving is blue
Pink is the passion
Red—I love you

Purple divine
Brown is the rain
Black is the heart of evil
Again

Yellow the sun
Up in the sky
White is the purest
Of colors combined

Color my world
Orange me too
Any way you look at it
It's eyeball hue

Tracey Travis Lee
Perryville, MD

Penn's Woods

Tall stands of forest, fifty feet high
with no undergrowth.
White-tailed deer have eaten all the new growth.
There are more deer now
than in William Penn's time.

Autumn colors are turning,
gold and cinnamon, yellow ochre.
Hawk and turkey vulture float in a cobalt sky.
A brook shimmers in the sunlight,
flowing down to the Brandywine.
A doe and two fawns drink warily.
They know the huntsmen are in the woods.

Cynthia Knuth Fischer
West Chester, PA

Sixteen Candles

I loved you from the moment
the doctor said that I was pregnant.
I held you close when you cried,
and rocked you to sleep at night.
I started calling you
"My little man" when you were two.
Now I think of you every day
and pray that you are safe.
It seems like only yesterday,
but my baby turns sixteen today!

Sandra Widner
Bainbridge, GA

Our Endless Love

Dedicated to my one true love

Our endless love began with just one little kiss,
A sweet, innocent 'n' gentle, unthreatening first kiss,
Like the first flowers pushing their tender stems above the ground.
Could this be the beginning, of innocence in love found?
The gentle cradling, of my hand in yours
Showed me the gentle touch and the beginning of true love.
Just as those young flowers slowly reached
For the orange glow of the sun,
We took our time 'n' nurtured the unique feelings that now had begun.
Just as the growing flowers began to bud,
So thus was our rapture being guided from above.
As the buds of the flowers started to bloom into a beautiful bouquet,
So does the beginning of our endless love begin today
As we put one another's desires and dreams before our own,
Now set into perpetual motion, our two hearts beat, but now as one.
Long ago a friendship had started, then turned to a romance
That was set afire,
All the longing we felt, our souls intertwined as our love began to Soar
even higher.
Our love showering down with heavenly stardust from the Milky Way,
Oh, how our love deepens, with the opening of each brand-new day.
An overwhelming completeness we do feel,
Just the way two lovers should,
Just one sweet innocent kiss turned into our endless love
Just as our hearts knew it would.
Oh, how mighty a sweet, innocent, 'n' gentle unthreatening first kiss.

Elaine Johnson
Rockledge, FL

The Orange Poem

In my mind there's a town
This town is called Orange
People walk around wearing different shades of orange
Magazine covers never print the skies of Orange
And from treetops down—you guessed it—orange
Ice cream is free on the corners of Orange
Butterscotch and chocolate never taste like orange
Lemonade and milk are packed with pride to pour orange
Every steak and lobster on the grill glows orange
Definition TVs all pinpoint orange
Captured with oil and ink raw orange
Stained glass windows give us see-through orange
While the valley down below boasts a blue-grassed orange
Birds in the giant orange trees display orange
Soldiers who fight overseas protect Orange
Teachers with chalk put down ancient Orange
So kids in class will know the history of Orange
Seasons come and go as the clocks tick in Orange
On Sundays you can hear steeple bells chime for Orange
Hay made with clover blankets the citizens of Orange
Sadly there are kids who think and dream of leaving Orange

Greg Randall
Springville, IA

Currently, I am getting older in the Midwest as I continue to escape the idea of growing up. One day, I was told of a poem writing contest. How cool would it be, I thought, to write a poem based on a word which cannot be rhymed? "The Orange Poem" soon took its first breath and I thank you for reading it. Never be afraid to enter a contest or do whatever it is you do. Always remember . . . you are a unique individual, just like everyone else!

Behold and Beware

Beauty to behold
Certain things may unfold
It's been days things still untold
It's a thousand years old
It's been a long time
Since sunshine
I still remember
Falling in love was like falling timber
It's been a while
Seeing her smile
The world was made to bring about love
Warm feelings in a lady's heart are beyond and above
Behold and beware
It is such a time people shall care
Never dare and neither swear
Having feelings to share, but may compare
Deep down somewhere
I prefer only her
Good things soon occur
Please behold something is bold and precious like gold
Wonderful days waiting ahead
Like sleeping dead, breaking bread
Happy things are waiting to be said
Behold and beware, take care

James Alexander
Laneville, TX

My Daddy

This story's about my daddy, indeed
Whom I will always love and need.
He's not just an ordinary man, you see
He's good as gold, especially to me.

He never complains. He takes everything well,
Even though I've put him through a lot of hell.
He's understanding, patient, kind, and sweet.
His love for his family can't be beat.

Time has passed and we kids are all grown,
But there's so many things we didn't make known,
Like how much we love him and how much we care,
And if ever he needed us, we would be there.

I envy my daddy for his strength
And to be like him, I'd go to any length.
He did his best to give advice
So we would grow strong, healthy, and wise.

There's always something I wanted to do,
Just go up to him and say I love you!
But things like that are hard to say.
I guess I'll just show him in my own special way.

Andrea Rogers
Big Sandy, TX

Journey of the Bridal Path

Mountains crumble 'neath the sky
The Earth, she whispers silent cries.
Only we, the ones to blame
For this we've done and feel no shame.
Light fades as days encompass me
Ash and dust fill land and sea
Mother Nature lashes out violently
Diseased by our painful greed
Failing to think of what will be.
Narrow is the weak of mind,
Mustn't be caught left behind.
Quakes and plagues will frail the spoil.
See now, and purge your heart
Doubt will only tear you apart.
There comes a time to make your choice
Speak aloud, He gives you voice.
Pride and lust only urge your fall.
Choose life now,
And have it all.

Stacey R. Walters
Gladewater, TX

I feel that God, through His divine Holy Spirit, motivated me to pen this work in hopes that it will change something or someone along their journey as well. Past mistakes and decisions as a society cannot be erased, but used rather as a tool to create a better future for us all. Everyone has freewill to choose this life. I don't remember when I became saved. However, I remember it was my Jewell that led me to the Lord. This poem is for my Lord and Savior, a gift for Him as He gave me, eternally.

Friend

Friend! Friend! Friend!
What does a friend means to you?
What is a friend?
Do you have a clue?
A friend can be an animal
That is easy to take care of
It can be a bunny or fish
Mostly a cat or a dog
It can be anything above
A pet is something to love
A friend can be a parent
Or someone you know
Someone who is there for you
Or someone who has a clue
A friend won't judge you
They will accept you the way you are
Whether you have faults or not
They like you for who you are
A friend is always there for you
Through good times and bad
They will even try to cheer you up
When you are sick or sad
A friend is someone to hang out with
Or talk to on the phone
Aren't you glad to be not alone?

Sonya L. Powell
Melbourne, FL

The Garden

For the garden of your daily living,
Plant three rows of peas:
Peas of mind
Peas of heart
Peas of soul.
Plant four rows of squash:
Squash gossip
Squash indifference
Squash grumbling
Squash selfishness.
Plant three rows of lettuce:
Lettuce be faithful
Lettuce be patient
Lettuce be playful.
No garden is complete without turnips:
Turnip for meetings
Turnip for service
Turnip to help one another.
To conclude our garden, we must have thyme:
Thyme for each other
Thyme for family
Thyme for friends
Thyme for God.
Water freely with patience and cultivate with love.
There is much fruit in your garden
Because you reap what you sow.

Anthony Nnatu
Chicago, IL

Remembering Charlotte—3/13/04

She drop-kicked her own grief
to help others cope with theirs.
She knew they could not forget,
neither would she.
So in his memory,
she planted a tree
near his favorite playground
where dimpled white balls
commanded the landscape.
He would be watching, she knew,
as a Tiger-drive sailed past
its tallest branches,
or a duffer's ball rolled gently
in its shade.
She has joined him now in
his spectator sport,
as we remember
in life, she planted more than a tree.

Kate Doyle Veckey
Chicago, IL

Where Is She?

Where is my mom? I need to know
Her mind is in the long ago.

Where is my mom? I see her here
I don't know if her thoughts are near.

They seem to flit and wander wide
I forced a smile—but then I cried.

I cannot bear to see her go
Into a world so sad, so slow.

I didn't know, I didn't see
I guess I hid from reality.

But now I know—what can I do?
She's here, but gone to a place that's new.

Sharon Jacobson
Schaumburg, IL

Strangers Are Friends

We haven't met
God knows
No strangers
He loves us all,
The poor, the rich,
The great, the small
He is a friend
Who is always there
To share our troubles
And lessen our cares
No one is a stranger
In God's sight,
For God is love
And in His light
May we, too, try
In our small way
To make new friends
From day to day
So pass no stranger
With an unseeing eye,
For God may be sending
A new friend by.

Joseph Nnamah
Chicago, IL

Oh, Death, Where Is Your Sting?

Life is short and death is sure;
The hour of death remains obscure.
A soul you have and only one.
If that be lost,
All hope is gone.
Waste not your time
While time shall last,
For after death, 'tis ever past.
The all-seeing God
Your judge will be,
Heaven or Hell, your destiny.
All earthy things will fleet away.
Eternity will ever stay.
And to console is an act,
The most sublime charity.

Stella Nwabueze
Chicago, IL

My World

The leaves are turning colors, they're starting to fall,
days and nights feel the same.
As I travel down this long road, the tears begin to fall like rain.
So why did you have to go and leave my world, my world?
I want someone to love me, someone to care about me.
You gave me a true smile, now it's just a mask.
So why did you leave my world?
Now that you're gone, the sun doesn't shine
and stars don't sparkle in my world.
Not my world.
Now I listen to my iPod,
not to drown out my thoughts
but to drown out your voice, your laughter, your happiness.
I want it back in my world. I want to create that laughter
and get rid of this mask.
I want a real smile.
So why did you leave my world?
Now that you're gone, the sun doesn't shine
and the stars don't sparkle in my world.
Not in my world.
The secret's out, there's nothing to hide now.
The way you look at me and the words you use to describe me,
they break my heart.
That's who I was, not who I am.
Everyone makes mistakes, and I admit I did,
and that's why you left my world, my world.

Emily Thuerauf
Ely, IA

I am seventeen years old. I live on a farm and enjoy working with all our animals. I show cattle and I also love sports. I used to play basketball and soccer, but unfortunately, I had a basketball injury and had to have two knee surgeries. The last was a total reconstruction. I wrote this poem, "My World," because my four best friends walked out on me. I was lost and alone everywhere I went, but my therapy was writing. I wrote down all my thoughts. God bless all, and thank you for reading my poem.

The Game of Life

What to do
When you don't have a clue
What's going on
Do you just hold on
For the ride
The game
It's all the same
'Cause there's nothing you
Can do
When you've got no clue
This life twists and turns
And often hurts when
It burns
Inside and out
And filled with doubt
You frantically search
For the way out
So I tell you now
It's time to learn how
To find the clue
Decide what to do
'Cause in the game of life
It's all up to you!

Sheryl Entrekin
Temple, GA

Survivors

Rats
Roaches
Debtors
Flies
And women

Martha Persley
Grandview, MO

Beautiful Things

Life is full of beautiful things.
The blooms on the roses,
you know that it's spring.
The first birds returning
up in my tree.
They seem to be singing their
songs just for me.
The beauty surrounds me
on most everything,
from the grass at my feet
to the clouds up above.
The world's surrounded
by the beauty of love.

Gloria Pfister
Gray Court, SC

Reflections

The day was cloudy
All around it was dull
So there she sat wondering
What was going on?
She was very depressed
And the atmosphere made her think
And thinking deep her thoughts went on to life
What life meant, what's its purpose
Then what happens after life?
Suddenly she started thinking
Who will attend my funeral?
She was healthy, no ailment or anything
There she lay lifeless
Had worked hard all her life
Always with a smile
Ready to help anytime, anyone
Her husband was shocked to see her lifeless
He was thinking how to spend the rest of his life without her
He was more in his thoughts and loss
She had children, grown up and on their own
They cared for her in their own way
She had a lot of friends
All had good thoughts about her
But too busy in their own way
Who will attend her funeral?

Ansuya Phadnis
Fremont, CA

Food for Thought

I can give you all my love, but it won't come quick
See, I can hold you though it all, but first answer me this
Would you love me as a vagabond, a nomad with no home
Or what if I didn't trust a soul, and never spoke a tone
Would you love me standing three foot six, and couldn't lift a finger
Or what if I could leave a room, but yet my smell would linger
Though you ain't gotta answer now, it's merely food for thought
But if I was lonely in the rain, then would you let me walk
What if I lost all my limbs, became a convalescent
Or if I couldn't keep a steady mind without anti-depressants
Could you take the good knowing the bad, or would it break you down
If I was to tell you all my pain, then would you still be down
See, you ain't gotta answer now, it's merely food for thought
I'd rather that you take the time to think before you talk
Now if I didn't know a thing, then would you love me still
Or what if I could never lead because I had no will
Would you love me in my lowest times, or merely in the highs
Or what if I couldn't deal with pain, so all I did was cry
Know you ain't gotta answer now, it's merely food for thought
But if I had to steal to live, then what would be your thoughts
Would you see me as a criminal, a man who has no heart
Or merely as a broken soul who travels through the dark
Could you love me as an infant does, or tell me, would it change
The second that you figured out I'm not the man inside your brain
Now if you couldn't deal with this, then go ahead and walk
But you ain't gotta answer now, it's merely food for thought

Steven C. May
Kansas City, MO

Thankful

My gears have been stripped and I'm stuck in one place,
And for a time I am sidelined
From the human rat race.
I sit in my chair with my leg propped up high
And look out of the window
As the days go by.
My cast is all colored in gayest array
With pictures, designs,
And nice things people say.
I have time to reflect on events of the past
And think of the friendships
So tried, true, and fast.
Expressions of sympathy, concern, aid, and help
Fill my heart with warmth,
Gratitude, and wealth.
For the phone calls, the flowers, the food, cards, and cheer,
I'll be eternally grateful
For many a year.
God's blessing upon you as you travel your way,
And may He be with you
Throughout every day.

Sarah D. Houseknecht
Carlisle, PA

Things That I Know

I know machines
And many other things.
I know all the players' numbers
And falling lumbers.
I know sports
Not measuring quarts.
I know fishing on a lake
Not about earthquakes.
I know hot cheerleaders
Not civil war leaders.
I know about bailing hay
Not about the bombing of the Hawaiian bay.
I know drums
Like a alcoholic knows rum.

I am
Who I am
There's no changing me.
You get what you get I am
What you see.

Michael Notaro
Cumberland, OH

Spring

Springtime is golden.
Warm air from the sun.
The air and the sun helps
the flowers bloom.
Rain moistens the ground to help
the blooms and roots to grow.

Spring is on March twenty-first.
People are cleaning their yards and homes.
Children are riding their bikes.
Having picnics at the parks.
Flying kites. Springtime is golden.
Couples are walking hand in hand,
planning weddings and falling in love.
Spring is golden. The warmth is so wonderful.
Bees are buzzing and collecting
pollen to make honey.
Spring is golden.

Patricia Sims
Davenport, IA

Pondering

So I sit here and wonder to myself
Why couldn't it have been someone else
The pain I feel (excruciating)
Like one day it will never heal
I have a lot of regrets
Not one day I wake up and I am not upset
Sad to say that it happens at least four times a week
Occasionally I'm still crying myself to sleep
Because of the beatings, the rape
I have realized now that I have built up so much hate
Talking about it, for me, that's a long shot
Because when I wake up, the memories still have me in a knot
You don't understand
I feel my life was in their hands
Every kick, every putdown, every punch
At the time all I wished was that my life was undone
You can tell me every day that I will be okay
Even suggest that I pray
And not one day I will believe
That my pain will be free of me
Yet minute by minute and day by day
I look for hope in every possible way
I try to be positive and consistent
Hoping that one day I will ask for assistance

Mishaela Taylor
Modesto, CA

My Name Is HIV

I am the Grim Reaper, the dream keeper. The
Needle digs deeper and deeper into the veins of
An addict as I slowly begin to multiply. I am
The reason why millions of people die a year; I
Am the epitome of fear. I wait here in the
Body of a young woman who doesn't remember
The man five years ago who was too damn fine
To wear a condom, and he sure as hell don't
Remember her.
Hello, my name is HIV. I am the girl
Next door. I am the boy selling dope down
The street. I am everywhere; in your churches,
Your schools, your homes. I spread through prisons
Like famine.
I am the blood of the crack babies born
To infected mothers that breast feed. My
Name is HIV. I don't care about your
Race, your income, or age. I make six
Figures, I make minimum wage.
I am your best friend, your husband,
Your children! I rip through South
Africa heartlessly. I am the new apartheid.
I cannot be subsided. I divide life into
Death. I am the Grim Reaper, the devil's keeper,
The silent weeper. Smart girls like you can't
Get HIV. Cute boys like them don't have HIV. Cool
Girls like me can't get HIV, right? Check your statistics!

I'Ketta Sierra James
Titusville, FL

I am twenty-one years old. I started out writing short stories when I was eight, and I began writing poetry when I was twelve. I was very shy and quiet, so writing was an outlet for me. Poetry was my way of expressing myself without speaking. Now that I am older, I want to be heard in hopes of inspiring others with my words. I like to write about things that people generally do not want to hear about because it's either too painful or too real, which is why I was inspired to write "My Name Is HIV." I am an open-minded, creative, and outspoken young woman with dreams of having some kind of impact on this world by having a pen, paper, and a voice.

Broken Dreams

Sweet dreams
From broken souls
Vacant spaces
And black holes.

Opened hearts
From tender lies
Silly fools
And crying eyes.

Strong denial
From lying faces
Lonely rooms
And empty places.

Scarred hopes
From burning pain
Useless stress
And needless strain.

Broken pieces
From shattered glass
Maybe this too
Will come to pass.

Diane Hawkins
Huntsville, AL

God's Smile

I wake up happy as can be,
for God is smiling down on me.
My heart on wings doth fly
o'er the mountains and 'cross the sky.
The smell of flowers everywhere,
I have no worries, I have no cares.
My life is truly blessed, you see,
for God is smiling down on me.

Freda C. Rochon
Concord, NH

A Long Road Home

The wind's coarse howl
eerily moaned
perhaps lamentations
for the dead (so many)
afore gone weary
of the struggle
for their (daily) bread
Oh to calm the tempest's fury
unto the garden we reclaim
bringing fruit to prosper
for our life
afore our enemies' reign

Marilyn N. Winter
Toms River, NJ

On Dipping Snuff

My mama, that's my grandma,
Was a smart lady as you'll soon come to see
She dripped Sweet Railroad snuff
Boy, did that look good to me
When I was four or thereabout,
I went to Mother and said I wanted to dip
She went in a rage and 'bout did a flip
But Mama said, "Oh, sure, I'll get you a can and a brush
Then we'll dip and rock and we won't have to rush"
Now you get a lot on a brush, then pop it right in yo' mouth
That's the way you do it down here in the South
Oh, what a surprise came to me
That stuff wasn't as good as I thought it would be
Mama said, "Don't fret, all you need is another dip"
One more dip was all I needed to make me see
Dipping snuff sho' wasn't for me
Now wasn't Mama smart to let me try that stuff
'Cause that fixed me on dipping snuff!

Nancy Harrison
Rocky Mount, NC

Lord Is My Strength

Lord is my strength and power
When I lost hope, You gave me
a touch and You whispered into my
ears and told me that everything
is going to be all right
You told me to trust in You only and I did
because Your love is strong
I don't have dreams,
I have faith in You, Lord
When everyone turns
their backs on me, You are still there
I thank You for giving me
power, love, faith, hope, strength,
and understanding
I call on You all the time
When I lost my child, Kenya,
didn't no one understand what I was
feeling but You, Lord
You held my hand so close to You
I felt Your power and Your love
I am so thankful for You, Lord
I am lost without You
Thank You for Your strength, Lord
and love, power, hope
The Lord is my strength.

Ella J. Cox
Morrow, GA

The Confession, in Writing, of a Passion

Dedicated to Countee Cullen, one of my favorite poets

Lord knows I've had this longing in my soul for the longest time.
My childhood days and dreams of it flow
like the rhythm of a river in the memory of my mind.
So I set sail in constant quest of my heart's desire
to make my dreams come true.
I feel the pulse of it, the nearness of it
here, in my gut, where the depth of it comes through.
And I wonder, after all these years of being solitary and alone,
after all these years of burning for the yearn
and as the flame has grown,
how much of a good thing is lost when passion flames into nova,
and if the price of the burn was worth the cost . . .
when there could be no other?

John C. Quesenbury
Colorado Springs, CO

Dreams of a Cat

Silently, silently
Slowly, slowly
I creep nearer
My prey still in sight
Silently silently
Slowly, slowly
I prepare to pounce
I lunge forward, my teeth sink in
Bong, bong
Bang, bang
I awake
My prey is gone
Bong, bong
Bang, bang
Here and there they run about
I close my eyes, it will soon be over
Silently, silently
Slowly, slowly
All are gone
Except my prey
Chirp, chirp
Rustle, rustle
I start to creep
My fun has just begun

Tiffanie Sojka
Denton, TX

Happiness

Happiness is something more
Than what a man lays by in store
More than prestige, more than power
Or fleeting pleasures by the hour

Happiness is kindness living
In friendly hearts in selfless giving
A will to feel with one another
And treat a neighbor as a brother

It is faith the nobler plan
That seeks the good in every man
That leaves all censure unexpressed
Forgives the flaw and sees the best

Happiness is gold refined
Within the heart a state of mind
No need to travel near or far
You seek and find it where you are

Lena T. Young
Warwick, NY

Venus Ascending

Under the moon the limbs of trees
cross each other like legs
longing for a lover's touch.
A breeze heavy with the scent of snow
dances wearily through restless bushes,
winter passes silently.
The wind and the rain embrace
the ground is a beating heart
the earth trembles with spring.
Under the rising sun
in the damp shadows of the roots and their trees
a promise lingers, Venus ascending.
She stretches with aching arms.
She longs to dance with summer.
Her blushing petals sweetly beckon lovers.
The hummingbird is a wise zen master
he sips from life but never drinks;
the bees hum, with envy.
They dance with the wind, they drink of each other.
She cannot go, her home is in the ground.
He cannot stay, his home is the wind and sky.

Phillip J. B. Pursell
Charlotte, NC

And Every Angel Cries

In life there is no sadder sight
then when those glor'ous orbs so bright
those gilded suns of human fears
dissolve so readily to tears.
Heaven's nymph the mind beguiles
and stops the heart when she smiles,
but when from clouded eyes cascade
sorrows behind her masquerade.
The angel sits, alone, confined
plagued by the horrors of her mind.
Beautiful down to her soft heart
but with her prison, she can't part.
She's pure of heart, and pure of soul
though mental beatings take their toll.
Hands outstretched with aid to give
beckoning the angel to live.
Her wings, though chained, she longs to fly
and to help the others reach the sky.
She must accept her life's true call
and rise against tormentors all.
Before another tear you shed,
pick up your sweet angelic head.
Ne'er shall the angel cry again,
nor suffer more heart-wrenching pain.
Your wings will stretch with strength of flight.
Your heart will soar, freedom's delight.

Bryan Scharf
Bright Waters, NY

Dream

Today, there are many leaves soaring through the sky'
Therefore, my soul is falling
Does anyone know that my soul suffers from sadness and loneliness?
There is much wind today,
So I sent my soul to soar with the leaves to land somewhere randomly
Somewhere someone will receive my infected soul
And understand my feelings
Today, there is also much sunshine
I dreamed that at the beach a golden-haired person received my soul
Oh, how I wished to touch that hair, to know and experience that
person
Tomorrow will not be windy or sunny
It will be rainy and miserable
It returns my soul cleansed from the infection
Though no longer sad, I become anxious and envious to miss
That person I do not know.

Autumn Rose
West Melbourne, FL

Love, Life, Loss

To live is to be lost.
Lost in love,
Lost in life,
Lost with curiosity,
Lost in love
When you see the one you love.
And your heart feels as if it is going to beat right out of your chest.
You feel that if that special someone were to leave,
You would lose everything.
Loss,
"You never know what you had until it is gone."
To lose something that is really close to you
Is a heartache that will only go away in time.
It takes time to heal,
It takes time to succeed,
But I am still here,
Time is all I need.
Moving on is starting over completely.
The start of something new is refreshing,
But it also gives you more temptation to mess up.
We all make mistakes in life,
All it means is we just have to get back up and try again.
Persistence is what keeps us motivated.
Never give up.

Annie Mills
Garden Grove, CA

Many things inspired my writing, my everyday trials, the reality I had to face. Most of all, when my world came crashing down, this poem held my truths and my whole heart. I put all my effort into this poem, and looking back, it reflects on myself as a person. I'm glad I wrote it. I love to write, and poetry is one of my favorite things to write because it gives me the freedom to express myself with a mysterious rhythm.

For Aidan

Teddy bears, trains, and cars
An angel's room
Orange, blue, green, and yellow
An angel's room
Close your eyes, dream sweet dreams,
Walk in gardens,
Playgrounds, and wonderlands
And me,
Me, from far away, I watch you
And when you cry
I want to fill the rivers and oceans
With my tears
And when you laugh
I want to move the Earth with my laughter
Give me your little hand
And let's walk together forever.

Cindy Pagiatakis
Plymouth, MA

This Journey

This journey called life that we are on,
Soon it will pass, then be gone.
We meet many people along the way,
Some we connect with, some we push away.
The adventures we have are of many sorts,
We stop and we go through a number of ports.
When we truly connect with the world around,
We make some friendships that most have not found.
This journey takes courage and strength to get through,
The people around us learn from us too.
We don't know when this journey will end,
Just make life its best, even sometimes pretend.
We all have the tools to survive the same,
For some it's a struggle to win the game.
We enter this journey without a clue
Of what life is, or what we should do.
Along our way, we live and learn
That what choices we make are of great concern.
To do the right thing, we don't always know,
Some things change quickly, some very slow.
The people we meet, the places we see,
Are all part of this journey for you and me.
The ones we connect with will always be there
To help us through with support and care.
Always stay focused on the journey you're on,
Soon it will be over, and all will be gone.

Norma Lopez
Billinge, MT

Untitled

Enter the atomic winter
dive into the rivers of needles and lies just to
salvage another's one life.
Return to the wildfires, retrieve the ashes.
Stare at the plane as it crashes, transforming life
into ashes.
Return to bullet storm, and claim your loved
one's corpse because that would have been what he
wanted,
or else for the rest of your days by guilt be
hunted.
Donate your blood to the masses, then observe
how much time passes
before you receive currency in return.
Then throw it into the fireplace and
watch it burn.
That's how you learn, that's how you learn how
to love. That's how you learn to hate.

Angel Saldana
Log Lane Village, CO

Our Last Embrace

I enter the room
A sense of death does loom.
Watching from across the way
Your eyes filled with pain.
Oh, how will I bear it
Not to see you again.
By your side, I do sit
A candle burns
The room dimly lit.
Clasping your hands in mine
A quiet prayer for more time.
My darling, he says to me
I love you always
Death will not keep us apart
For you are my soul, my heart.
My dearest, I whisper
Forever will I love only you.
Do not leave me, I silently cry
Unbearable the sorrow becomes.
As the tears run down my face
We share our last embrace.

Lisa Wiles
Richmond, VA

My name is Lisa Wiles. I live in Richmond, VA, with my two wonderful children and five pets. I enjoy writing poetry, especially love poems. I was inspired to write this poem by my strong belief in soulmates and that true love is forever.

Mama

Mama, I'm trying, but it's getting so hard, you see.
You're not here with me.
Woke up this morning, thought I heard you calling.
Sounds in the kitchen with pots and pans, baking that cake.
"Baby girl! Where did I put that pot?"
"What would I do without my baby girl!"
We shared so much, you and me over the years . . .
Why did you have to leave?
Sharing memories of your childhood with me.
Such a beautiful child—a child of God you truly are,
Always giving to others and making them happy.
Baking those homemade cakes, giving away more than you sold . . .
"To give is better than to receive" I was always told.

You and your "salt of the Earth" ways,
In this age we live makes me yearn for the good old days.
Your love of fishing, the simple things in life,
Loving your brothers and sisters was always a treasure
That you held dear . . . family first was always your pleasure.

I'll never live up to the woman you were, but Mama, I'm trying.
You have so many friends in Heaven, but I'm here without you.
On this uneven playing field, I want to be strong, but losing ground.
Mama, reach down and show your baby girl the way that's true.

Violet Van Schuyver
Harrisburg, NC

God Is Here for Us

God is here for us
When we all need
Him in our lives.

God is here for us
When we are in
Trouble.

God is here for us
When we have terrible things
Happen in our
Lives.

God is here for us
When we need Him
To pray and talk
To Him about
Our problems
And the stuff
We do.
God is here for us
When we pray
To Him.

Mattie Lindsay
Fulton, MO

Shining

When the world seems like a lonely place
No one there to call and help you face
Your problems through

There's a special aura in the air
The love we carry and we share
Is the secret part of you

The power's with you
Just let it shine through
Shining brightly on you
You can make it too

When you wonder what's your rightful place
The things we do just show mistakes
Life's shining on you
Soon you will make it too

I'm depending on you
To see yourself in full view
The powers with you
Shining shining for you

Yvette Denise Lee
Independence, MO

Underrated Moms

The bond of love
Between a child and mother,
Together they make
A match like no other.
Just a stay-at-home mom,
That's so not true.
Do we ever consider
Everything they do?
They're nursemaids and doctors,
And sometimes advisers,
Housekeepers, chefs,
And taxi drivers.
Kids don't come with instructions,
Manuals, or books,
But moms just know
When to give you the look.
But just a housekeeper
Is the only title they get.
They're domestic engineers,
Now doesn't that fit?

Fran Kalebaugh
Laurie, MO

December Words

I'm nervous to ask, I'm not sure what to say.
I just think about you and I hope you're okay.
I can't sleep at night, and awake I lay.
You'd be with me, if I had my way.
I fall asleep in hopes you'll still be
Alive and well, and here with me.
I think of myself, too blind to see,
And in my dreams, you slowly leave.
And I'm so afraid that it's not a dream,
That everything's not what it seems.
These worries in mind, and our memories I keep,
And if something should happen,
I hope I'm asleep. I don't trust God,
But I stop and pray that I would know
You're alive today. If ever God
Should take you away, in my heart
You'll always stay. I hope all day
And at night I pray that when I wake,
You'll be okay.

Jalyssa Rogers
Bunkerville, NV

I'm Tired, I'm Done!

I'm tired of me.
I'm tired of life.
I'm tired of trying so hard.
I'm tired of helping.
I'm tired of fighting.
I'm tired of taking responsibilities that
aren't even mine.
I'm tired of people.
I'm tired of liars.
I'm tired of being called things I'm not.
I'm tired of downs.
I'm tired of lows.
I'm tired of idiots.
I'm tired of losers.
I'm tired of being betrayed even by
my "best friends."
I'm tired of hiding.
I'm tired of everything.
I'm tired of it all.
I'm done.

Leslie Miles
Homosassa, FL

Criticism

Getting criticized all your life hurts like hell,
and when the pain hurts so bad,
who are you supposed to tell?
I should know because I got
criticized all of my life,
and those mean and hateful words
still hurt like a sharp knife.
This type of cycle never seems to come to an end,
but through it all, I had just one good friend.
You try going through life where you can't walk right,
and whenever people start making fun of you,
that's when you wished you were out of sight.
So I'm just thankful to have God in my life because I know
that He won't criticize me for anything that I do wrong,
and in my heart is where He will belong.

Michelle L. Williams
Jacobsburg, OH

Brenda

In her role as a beautician,
Brenda wears many hats.
She listens, offers suggestions,
She laughs and things like that.

Lots of things she has to do,
She easily manages two boys and a husband, too—
Homework, football, weddings, spring break,
A grandson right on cue—
This is just to name a few!

But her customers have nothing to fear
She is very efficient, such a dear.
She pampers, perms, cuts, colors, and shampoos.
There's really not much that she cannot do!

She always greets you with a smile,
Never forgets to say goodbye.
It's a true fact—Brenda is not really a magician,
But our therapist, our friend, and one classy beautician.

Christine C. Lusk
Epps, LA

Startled Glances

5:34 a.m., Thursday, and one startled glance
Into a mirror left a once-gentleman shaken as
He sees someone he never knew, an
Apparition within a deeply entrenched mist
Treading upon a cobbled road of imagined terror
Destination: only a puddle of white-hot anger
In which to bathe
One startled glance at the growling dog
Between his feet with haunches high left him
Wondering, what if these sisters were relics
Unknown for such a secluded time as to come as
One more surprise from the not-so-near future
Perhaps not
Somewhere among the blue tiles come whispers of
"You are unique, yet entirely different from
Your youthful doppelganger, and
Quite possibly, not what you have
Yearned to be, at least not since the
Crocuses were last in bloom"
And with yet another startled glance, the
Dog has disappeared, and only a disinterested
Shrug could be mustered as
He continues to brush his teeth

William Santos
Boca Raton, FL

Table Conversation at My Grandfather's

***Dedicated to Vivi, my grandparents, my Opa and his parents,
and to my Uncle Gideon***

Shh, don't speak so loud
He survived the Death March
Pinkowitz was in Auschwitz
Like your grandparents
But they were gassed
Yes, in forty-three
How did he survive?
They shot him
He laid in the ditch filled with bodies
They thought he was dead
He's crazy now
The kids are scared of him
Sometimes he talks to himself
Others, he just looks right through you
He probably would be better off dead
My uncle with the blue numbers on his arm
Says no one is better off dead.

Robert M. Leskovac
New York, NY

I Hate the Way

I hate the way I feel inside
Every time I see your face
I hate the way my heart starts racing
No matter the time and place

I hate the way you smile
And the way it makes me feel
I hate your beautiful eyes
I hate this whole ordeal

I hate the way I miss you
Especially when you walk by
I hate this lonesome feeling
I hate wondering why

I hate the way you smell so good
Under any circumstance
I hate the way it ended
I want one more chance

I hate the way I can't hate you
No matter how hard I try
I hate the way I can't have you back
No matter how hard I cry

Reba Powell
Monticello, MS

Sister, Sister

Oh, sister, sister, where might you be,
up in Heaven looking down on me?
Oh, how I wish you were here sitting
next to me.
Just like old times when we
would sit with our needles and thread,
sewing those tiny blocks together
with love in every stitch.
Oh, sister, sister, where might you be,
up in Heaven looking down on me?
I am still sitting in my chair with
my needles and thread sewing
those quilts like we once did,
but with every stitch I make, I look
over at the chair next to me,
but you're not there like once before,
and it brings tears to my eyes,
for I wish you were here sitting
next to me.
Oh, sister, sister, where might you be,
up in Heaven looking down
on me?

Margaret Breeden
Oak Ridge, TN

Who Am I?

I am winter. I am spring. I am peasant. I am king.
I am zero. I am nine. I am darkness. I am shine.
I am Satan. I am God. I am normal. I am odd.
I am ground. I am sky. I am low. I am high.
I am up. I am down. I am smile. I am frown.
I am living. I am dead. I am blue. I am red.
I am hatred. I am love. I am sword. I am dove.
I am spirit. I am walking. I am silent. I am talking.
I am father. I am son. I am nothing. I am one. I am torture.
I am fear. I am laughter. I am tear. I am beauty. I am beast.
I am most. I am least. I am chaos. I am fate. I am little.
I am great. I am water. I am wine. I am bothered. I am fine.
I am stupid. I am smart. I am mortal. I am art.
I am rich. I am poor. I am virgin. I am whore.

Nothing less and nothing more. Nothing less and nothing more.

I am everyone.

Ryan Albishi
Tulsa, OK

I Matter

I matter
I matter not because I'm rich or famous,
Not because I'm popular, or not that you
Even know me, I matter
To my sisters and my brother, to my mother, who
For whatever reason decided not to abort me
And suffer many months in pain to bring me
Into this world to mold me, shape me,
Put the fear of God in me, I matter
To Martin Luther King, Malcolm X, Rosa Parks,
Maya Angelou, and all the Black men and women
Who fought for me to have the freedom
That I now have, I matter
To my friends, my man, my son, and daughter
For whom I am responsible to create in them
Independence, love for their heritage, respect
For themselves and others, I matter
And last but not least, to myself, a woman
Who has overcome hardships like abuse,
Drug addiction, and homelessness because
I have the hopes, dreams, and potential to be
Whatever I want to be, I matter

Elyce F. Sweeting
Seattle, WA

Nature

Smell the air,
then touch the trees,
nature is endangered
and that's no tease.

Contractors and loggers have
to destroy our precious treasures,
they pave it over and
we lose our pleasures.

Nature is needed for
our wildlife,
tear down no more or
there will be no life.

Nature is open
and free,
a priceless gift to protect,
so look around and see.

Paula Alger
Gibsonton, FL

Mother's Day

A mother would give her life
So her child could live.
There is nothing like a mother
And the love that she gives.

How special it is to know someone who cares,
And will always be there
To give of herself each day she lives.
How lucky we are to have a mother.

When I think of all the things she did for me,
She taught me living, loving, and giving
That I will never forget.
Not only is she a wonderful mother,
She is a unique woman.

Let her know you appreciate her so
With unconditional love in your heart.
What amazing joy she will feel.
Of all the expensive gifts she may receive,
The miracle of love rules over all.

Happy Mother's Day
To mothers everywhere.

Genevieve Delp
Brighton, IL

Insomnia

Her head spins and she can't sleep
Life is a nightmare as the grim reaps
Doors slam, windows crack, mirrors break
And yet from this hell she cannot wake
Close her eyes and she's falling, falling
Her voice is gone, still they are calling
The voices scream and shriek her name
The voices with their whispers drive her insane
Continue falling, falling into the abyss
Maybe to be saved by death's kiss
Love is not a far enough escape from fear
As life spins in its circles, realities disappear
What is time that we are trying to kill
An empty soul that we desire to fill
The uncontrolled eyes snap open and are blinded
Picks herself up from the floor with hands binded
Her head pounds, another night without sleep
But the mask has been placed so she will not weep

Hannah Schiller
Coon Rapids, MN

My Brother Patrick

He was tiny and beautiful
This little baby boy
The day he was brought home
With excitement and joy
Did he see me, hear me
Know that I was there
How much I loved him
And just look at that beautiful curl in his hair
He could sing, he could dance
He was quite the little man
Just put on the music
For he was also quite the ham
We'd spend hours together playing Frank and Joe
Serving up much more than our "cocktails"
But memories, you know
Then there was basketball, baseball, and football too
And the girls with their crushes
Who'd bake cherry pies just for you
Then your journey through life truly began
And with all your accomplishments
I still see that little man
So bold and bright, right from the start
That little baby boy
That captured my heart

Michelle Profant
Goleta, CA

The Lord's Spirit

Lord, I felt Your presence here today
As I watched the winds, the branches sway.
I felt You in the clouds o'erhead
As misty rain on Earth was spread.

I felt You, Lord, when I looked out
And saw spring's robins hop about,
Then listen for their breakfast worm
As 'neath the ground they crawled and squirmed.

I heard the birds' sweet, cheery songs
That I had missed all winter long.
I saw some branches start to bud
And flower sprouts creep up through mud.

Your Spirit, Lord, is everywhere—
A blessing Lord, to know You're there
To lift our spirits, be our friend
And hear the prayers to You we send.

I felt Your Spirit in the air
And felt the love You gently share.
The clouds soon left, the sun shone bright,
Your Spirit, Lord, said, "All is right."

Eileen M. Taylor
Salem, OR

I was given a book of poems by Robert L. Stevenson when I was a child and I loved the poems, as they made me feel a part of them in many ways. In many of my poems, I find that putting myself "there," I get a better understanding and the words seem to find their way of expression. I feel God gave me the talent to use. I'm now eighty-eight, and He still guides and blesses me, as ideas on many subjects float through my mind in the form of a poem.

Dead End

In this serious
Rut
I'm hopelessly
Stuck
I'm not even exaggerating, I'm
Trapped
And the fact that I'm
Distracted
Doesn't help any more than I'm
Alone
Forget this, I'm completely
Done
Pitiful, so sorry, so
Sad
Finally realizing I'm better off
Dead
The
End

Angela Peteani
Yonkers, NY

Little Blossoms

It's been said that kids are rare flowers
In the garden of a parent's own heart
Bringing joy and smiles, and the sunshine;
Truly, God's blessing from the start.

These blossoms are many and are varied,
But each has its place in the soil,
And though it is work to help grow them,
Each flower is a reward of the toil.

And just as a flower has its beauty
And brightens the dullest of rooms,
So do the sweet little faces
Of those small, tender, dear little blooms.

How blessed is the home with these flowers!
How evident the favor of God.
So if you find there are some in your garden,
Care well for those blooms in the sod!

Kathy Chester
Mooresville, NC

The Dogs on the Yip Train Go to Disney World

Here comes the dogs on
the train going to Walt Disney.
We know someday they'll make history.
They go to visit Mickey and Minnie Mouse.
Mickey invites the dogs in
to visit his and Minnie's little cheese house.
The dogs wag their tails with so much pride
when Mickey and Minnie take them on the teacup ride.
The hobby horses take them
up and down and up and down,
and they enjoy the music on the merry-go-round.
They say goodbye to their little
mouse friends while they eat their cotton candy.
They tell their master they had more fun than Jim Dandy.
This just lets you know
that Disney World is fun from kids
and dogs from four to eighty-four,
and they'll always remember the boat ride
and hearing the song "It's a Small, Small World."
So get on the train and give it a whirl.

Carolyn A. Wentworth
Cleburne, TX

Winter's End

We sit and wait for the passing of time,
like a capsule that's buried or a cocoon to open and fly.
The days all pass, it's hard to see
just how long winter is to be.
Each winter different, some longer, it seems,
but this one continues with snow falling, you see.
What once was a beautiful blanket of white
now is a nuisance with no end in sight.
We struggle to make these days not so dark,
and cope with the snow that always leaves a mark.
Remember that patience is always a must,
and with the dawn always comes dusk.
This winter we'll remember most of all with dread,
and look forward to spring and warm weather ahead.

Hazel Jean Everett
St. Joseph, MO

This Tree Outside My Window

As I watch winter's nakedness,
I stay to see bumps of life
forming, swinging from each branch.
I stay and see bumps growing
into wide smiles, green in
color, preserved by this
bright sky ball holding the
position of mother.
I stay and see the changings
bursting into colors of red, yellow,
brown, and pale gold.
Graveyard awaits, each
color crisp and fall,
each in its own place.
I hear the wind howl through
the crack in my window as a
sign of bare branches coming.
I stay and watch, next time.
My tree, beautiful in all forms.

Geraldine Gipson
Chicago, IL

Child of Wonder

The wonder of it all
The songs of joy
The joy of giving
The laughter of children
Angels singing songs of joy
Angels praising God above
Angels spreading news of hope
Shining brightly in the night
Star of David shines so bright
Leading us to the manger
Where the child of wonder is born
Angels singing songs of joy
Angels praising God above
Angels spreading news of hope
The child of wonder is born
To bring peace and joy to Man
Oh, sing a song of joy
Oh, sing a song of hope
Oh, sing a song of peace
That's the wonder of it all
Angels singing songs of joy
Angels praising God above
Angels spreading news of hope

Debra D. Smith
Denton, TX

Love Me Please

Please make me laugh, never make me cry,
Please tell me the truth, never utter a lie.
Please hold me in your arms where I belong,
Please tell me our love cannot be wrong.
Please make me feel beautiful in every way,
Please love me more with each passing day.
Please show me your love with every touch,
Please say you'll always love me this much.
Please lend me a shoulder to shed a tear,
Please show me love and never any fear.
Please make me feel like I am the only one,
Please! I've never felt this way with anyone.
Please be the one to make me always smile,
Please be the one to go that extra mile.
Please show me passion in your every kiss,
Please show me eternal, loving bliss.
Please know that I love you more each day,
Please don't let anyone stand in our way.
Please know in my heart you are very near,
Please know in my soul our love is dear.
Please know that you are the one for me,
Please let me love you and you will see!

Christine L. Austin
Mesquite, NV

What Makes a Family?

What makes a family?
Is it growing up with a mom and dad?
Is it growing up with a single parent?

Could it be having parents who are male and female?
Could it be having parents who are of both sexes?

Maybe it's having grandparents step in
When times are hard

Maybe it's having an older brother or sister
Taking care of everyone

Maybe it's having two families
Come together as one

What really makes a family is having
Happiness, love, acceptance, cherished memories
And a special bond that lasts forever

Anita M. Jones
Milwaukee, WI

Moms

I traded eyeliner for dark circles.
Salon hair for ponytails and braids.
Designer purses for diaper bags.
Moms don't care what we gave up
and will continue to give up.

Tameka Abcumby
Waterford, MI

What's a Job?

Something I really hunger
So I continue to hunt
I apply for every possible spot
Not sure I even have a shot
So many people have the same intention
Gives me too much extra tension

A letter of words enhanced
To give me a better chance
My resume squeezed on a page
Hoping it gets me to the next stage
My career under review
Just wishing for that interview

Vicki Svir
Battle Ground, WA

The Broken Heart

Her heart in pieces was broken
By the harsh words he had spoken
"I'm going to leave you," he loudly said
"I almost wish you were dead"
"You've ruined my life, don't you see
Just by being tied to me
I'm going to find someone new
I don't care if it makes you blue"
He quickly turned and left the house
She went to their bedroom as quiet as a mouse
Her eyes were filled with big, hot tears
She hadn't cried like that in many years
She said a prayer to God above
And thanked Him for His matchless love
She prayed, please bring him back to me
For I still love him, don't you see
The very next month, he came back home
He had decided he didn't want to roam
He said, "Please forgive me, I love you still
We'll stick together, I know it's God's will"

Lou Ila Jenkins
Lindsay, OK

This Day

The sun is shining bright,
This day feels so right.
The sky is looking incredibly blue,
What a lovely view.
Birds are singing pretty sweet
Somewhere up in a tree.
Flowers are blooming here and there,
They'll quickly pick me up if I'm in despair.
I feel a kind of beauty in the air
That nothing in this world can compare.
It is heartwarming, soothing, and great,
Always real, never fake.
This day should never go away.
This day is lingering over the Maumee Bay.
My eyes see this day of delight,
I must keep this day until the night.
This day is changing into tomorrow
With lots of joy, no sorrows.
No clouds in the sky,
No tears to cry.
This day puts smiles on my face
And leaves me in a better place.
Breezes blowing all around
Make this day profound.

Arlene Harper
Toledo, OH

Beyond the Grave

There is a place beyond the grave.
There is a place where Jesus waits,
And when I reach those pearly gates,
There I will meet my Master face to face.
There is a place beyond the sky.
Why should I sit and cry,
Because I am going to see Him by and by.

Rose Mitchell
Downers Grove, IL

Jesus Wept

What do you/ewe have on Earth?
Testing of strife/tribulations or humbled joyful mirth?
Your life is what you/ewe make it to be
Confession of Jesus Christ resurrected or unrepentant misery.
Salvation, love, thanksgiving reign upon all who offend thee!

Your life not ever to be blamed on other's devil deeds,
Only God is love of fatherless/widows'/neighbors' needs.
Be patient, brothers and sisters, toward all men every day.
What do you/ewe have on Earth?
Holy Spirit boldness because "Jesus wept,"
The righteous "unceasingly pray."

Corinne Anne Callender Hoyt
Dowagiac, MI

Purpose

Through weather's scorn,
Tattered and torn,
A ray of colors can be seen.
Life held its destiny.
Now it holds its own.
It had no value, need,
Just a purpose.
Everything has a purpose,
Such as the kite!

Mary Ann Corey
Lorain, OH

Only You, Babe

After a night
of blissful affection
we rolled out of bed
toward separate rooms—
one for a cigarette,
one to the loo—
and a delight
beyond the others
was the companionable clunk
as we blundered into
different doorjambs

Jeanne T. Beatty
St. Thomas, PA

My Friend

All through the years she's been smiling
since the Savior set her free.
No matter what some folks may think,
He's real to her and me.
He's living deep within her heart,
and keeps her satisfied,
and always when she's needed Him,
He's right there by her side.
She's depending on His promises
to treat her tenderly,
so she lives to see the Master
smiling back with glee.
He's her friend when she gets lonely.
Oh, yes, He's always there.
He wraps His arms around her
to protect and show He cares.
And even in her darkest hours,
she feels Him oh, so near,
and knows that she can trust Him
to take away her fear.
She's depending on His promises
to treat her tenderly,
so she lives to see the Master
smiling back with glee.

Sylvia A. Godfrey
Tavernier, FL

Born in Washington, D.C. to loving parents who loved the Lord Jesus Christ, their fellowman, and music, my parents taught me to be caring, sharing, and to express myself in music. All of my poems are songs I've written about these attributes. This song is about my friend and prayer partner of thirty-plus years, Elaine Rigsby, who was a school librarian. A single lady, she was my dearest friend and supporter. She has gone to be with the Lord—I miss her—and this poem explains our friendship and beliefs.

Bedtime Story

Another night is here
The doorway, you appear
Here I'm lying scared
While you pretend you care
Your mind can only concentrate on getting what you need
Not knowing it's my dignity upon of what you feed
Each day I'm robbed of my pure soul or what of it remains
How dare you look into that mirror with every passing day
The time will come when you will lose
Your unclaimed, jaded glory
Till then, I will pray to God
Your untold bedtime story
Every day's unknown
Of how my heart has grown
Though others know it's real
Alone is how I feel
It shouldn't be so difficult to make this go away
If only they would see the pain within my eyes displayed
Each day I wonder how I'll survive with what is left remained
While others look into that mirror, not noting the disdain
Perception vows when time will pass
Your unclaimed, jaded glory
Till then, I will pray to God
Your untold bedtime story

Kristen N. Field
St. Charles, MO

Behind Rainbow

Behind rainbow is a land of puppies that angels take care of
and play with that is so beautiful, wonderful.
From time to time, angels let puppies out on Earth
to live about ten years to rescue, help humans
to escape stress, pressure.
These puppies are valuable, amazing making miracles
in all lives that they touch.
They have a joy, passion, vanishing stress,
pressure in people's lives like a beautiful sunny summer day.
Before they die and go back to Puppies' Land that is wonderful,
they touch, fill so many lives to have courage going deeper
in their heart, trusting, forcing on Lord Almighty.
To forcing, running toward their dreams,
smiling like a child on Christmas Day.
Expressing all their love out like beautiful, wonderful
sunny summer days in gifts that Lord had blessed them with.
Having courage, faith, being loyal, abeyance to the Lord
to develop your gifts to amaze, inspire, and surprise others.
Behind rainbow and in Heaven is a small land call Puppies' Land.
Puppies can sleep, eat, play all day and go down to Earth
from time to time to help vanish some of life's stress, pressure.

Dave J. Vickery
Chicopee, MA

My dog, Diamond, died in March 2010. I made a poem about her to touch,
encourage, and inspire others. Like a beautiful sunny day, she liked going for a
walk in all seasons at sunset. I have the privilege, joy, and gift to write a lot of
poems in all the seasons. I feel special and alive as I dream, writing a touching,
wonderful poem. As the sun sets and birds sing, it places my love in a beautiful
poem, lifting others back up to smile.

Theresa

Theresa, my love
You are now with Jesus in Heaven above
The Lord has come and taken you away
I ask Him why every night when I pray
In Heaven, you do not have one defect
Your eyes, mind, and legs are now perfect
You must be very happy in Heaven, my dear
But I am selfish and wish you were still here
I am left here with so much sorrow
Hoping it will be a little less tomorrow
No matter how much suffering and pain
Never did you complain
I was also afraid to die, but now I am not
To be with you again is the only hope I've got
When you said you would marry me, I was so glad
I thank God for the forty-seven years together we had
The best thing I ever done in my life
Was to take you for my wife
You were always so sweet and gentle as a dove
Theresa, my love

Chester R. Williams
Jewett City, CT

Rain

Children's excited breath blurs glass doors
Smiling eyes, equipped for hours of puddle jumping
That will only last five minutes
Duck boots a shade of sunflower yellow
While dank sky lies overhead
Rain drizzles on windows
A child's fingerprint lingers on the cold glass
And a tired mother gives in to her children's wishes
And ushers them outdoors
Minutes later, they return wet, cold, and eyes sparkling
The fresh scent of rain lingers in the air
Green leaves and pink flower petals glisten
Glycerin perfect drops lie undisturbed
And a slight wind blows
And the rain falls
Again, rain falls from the dank sky
Again, children beg parents for moments outside
Moments later, skies clear
Natural phenomenon: a rainbow
Light dances on colors in the sky
Our own frozen aurora borealis
Children stare with awe
Ready for tomorrow's spring rain

Meaghan M. Graham
New Market, NH

The Message

I received
The message He left for me
It said
He'd return when time
Ceased to be

I will ascend
Up by the throne in the sky
With my arms opened wide
To sit and hear the messenger
Will fill my heart

Of that I'm sure
To be accepted

You need only to ask
For that is His one greatest task

I will never forget
The message that day
When He said
I'm here to stay

Linda Fitzgerald
Dallas, TX

How We Pay Our Dues

You come along talking fancy,
you bring me wine and take me dancing.
I've played the game many times myself.
All the schemes and all the plans
aren't so hard to understand,
just wind them up and leave them on a shelf!
It's been done to you, it's been done to me,
and when it's done, it don't seem right.
The time we spend alone, we both feel used.
You pay for sunshine with the rain,
you pay for laughter with the pain.
Isn't it sad how we pay our dues?
You say there's a part of you
inside you naturally just have to hide.
We spend our lives in covering
a part of us that's smothering,
and it's easier to run than make a stand.
The ostrich hides its head in the sand,
and all this is according to God's plans.
The moral and the plot is
there's more to life than what we got!
Tell me, isn't it sad how we pay our dues?
And there's a light so bright
in me that it shines so bright in you.

Tonya Meyers
Sturgess, MI

After seeing family members and friends struggle through personal pain and tragedies in their lives, and seeing how their faith gave them the strength and courage to go on, I know that there is more to this life than just our own personal day-to-day struggles, and we can live an enlightened life. This is what inspired my poem.

Alone

This is the place that I call home,
There's only me—I live alone.

The time comes and the time goes
Where it goes, I'll never know.

I'm not happy, I'm not sad.

It's no mansion, it's no castle,
But yet, I love to be there.

I walk the path that brightens my day
As the warm sunshine guides my way.

My cares and worries just wash away

Each moment filled with knowing time,
I treasure each day that is mine.

The sun, the moon, each cotton cloud,
I feel all the joys that are allowed.

I find that I'm really not alone,
I love this place that I call home.

Donna Wrobleski
Benson, MN

Love Poem

I've been with you since the beginning
And have supported you all the way.
I've been waiting so long just to hear you say . . .

I've told you many times the way I feel
And how I want to show you that I'm for real.

For some reason which remains unknown
You don't feel the same; is your heart made of stone?

We're moving at a different pace,
It's moving so slow I rarely ever see your face.

Maybe it's me; am I moving too fast?
I want you, no one else; we don't need this supporting cast.

I say, "Let's do it before it's too late,"
You say, "Slow down, I think we should wait."

It's obvious your feelings aren't the same,
I sit here with no one but myself to blame.

Days pass and I want to be with you,
Suddenly, the phone rings; you say goodbye, farewell, adieu.

Caleb Schweer
Fresno, CA

Untitled

As I stand alone in the still of the night
And look to the heavens with stars so bright
The soft breezes blow a sweet refrain,
The sound of my Lord; did He call my name?
I hear the birds and the cricket sound,
All of the echoes of life abound
The heavens so lovely on this, such a night,
It's warm and quiet, and all seems so right
I think of His promise to always be here,
And know His voice is loving and clear
Sometimes we forget when the darkness rolls in,
But remember, in Jesus, we have a true friend
Just lean on His Word, we are never alone;
His commandments to us were written in stone
It seems all is lost if we lose our way,
But there's always the light at the break of day
Let's always be willing to fall on our knees,
To love Him and praise Him is sure to please
He rules the Earth and the heavens above
One day we'll go home to abound in His love
But today is a treasure, tomorrow, a gift
As the waters of life and sands, they sift
There is no room for doubt as we travel along,
So let's lift up our voices and sing a glad song

Joyce Floyd
Proctorville, NC

The Day America Will Never Forget

The tragedy of September eleventh two thousand one was one of horror
Leaving Americans asking why and worrying about tomorrow.
Terrorists captured planes and into the World Trade Center they hit
Without crew or passengers never knowing what unfolded in
The cockpit.
A seized plane blasted into Washington's Pentagon
And left people running for their lives
And wondering what was wrong.
There were those who crashed in Pennsylvania so brave
Fighting, willing to save others, maybe hundreds
More from the grave.
There were thousands who lost their lives that day
But through the wreckage, others were able to make their way.
Fireman and cops in service to others lost their lives
Leaving behind children, mothers, fathers and wives.
The President of our USA and New York City's mayor
With such pain and despair in their hearts
Led our nation through the disaster
With all the strength and courage that any human could master.
The tragic day of September eleventh two thousand one with much regret
Will go down in history as a day America will never forget.

Carolyn Councilman
Graham, NC

A Plan

When you have a negative thought
Something you wish was not
Use your remote to change your mind
And leave that thought behind.

Fill the space inside your head
With some happy thoughts instead.
Sometimes you have to use your brain
To solve some things that are a pain.

But when that job is done
Fill the space with something fun!
Laugh a lot and seldom cry.
You can get a natural high.

Do a favor for someone in need.
Be sure the laws you always heed.
Breathe deep and often every day.
It helps to keep stress at bay.

Think about what you have to say.
Do things in a kind and gentle way.
Soak up all the peace you can.
Now you really have a plan!

Arlene Andognini
Rowe, MA

Abundance

Many things in life, a shortage may be,
But those in abundance are usually free.

An abundance of rain, hushed is the sound,
Beautifully shatters as it hits the ground.

An abundance of light, perfect and pure,
Scatters the night, and our doubts are made sure.

An abundance of thought—free is our will
To ponder, reminisce . . . more is there still!

An abundance of pain—lost is this world,
Without love, without Christ, torment unfurled.

An abundance of hope for all of those
Who know the Savior, there is repose.

An abundance of grace, unworthy are we.
For us, Jesus died, and that, friend, is free!

Rebekah L. Campbell
Lebanon, VA

Frustrated

Frustrated, day by day.
Want to throw it all away.
This way of feeling is so old,
But not so bold.
I'm so young, supposed to be in the prime of my life,
Yet all I have is strife.
Frustrated, frustrated,
My pains make me so irritated
No one knows what it's like to be me.
What is it that you can't see?
I'm different in many ways.
This is my life every day.
When do I get a break?
Frustrated, stressed,
Makes me too depressed.
Living like this is a battle from within me.
This is not how it should be
For poor, old frustrated me.

Amy Marino
Ridgewood, NY

I wrote this poem because I suffer from fibromyalgia, and this describes my daily life. I'm twenty-five and live with my family in New York. My dad actually inspired me since I wrote a poem for him and read it at his funeral Mass. I also have a cat who is one of the most important things in my life outside of my friends and the New York Yankees.

The First Snowfall
Is Already Here

As the sun sets
across the yard,
all I can see is
a beautiful stream
of light,
'tis night.
Well, the sun is gone
and past,
it is night at last,
although I'd like to stay,
but now I really have to pray.
The sky turns black,
all I hear,
the first snowfall
is already here!

Sydney Seuntjens
Remsen, IA

Forever Palm

Here I stand bowed and swaying
Against the cold wind that pushes and molds me
Wondering each day what the next will bring
Can I withstand the raging hurricane
Blowing from one side of me to the other and on into the sea
How long can I hold in the passage of time
My past leaves mars I carry through my future
Mars that show I lived another life
How grand it would be to find a mate
Carried by a quiet summer wind
Dropped and rooted in this, my bay
Would my mate stretch open its limbs
Would it help me breach the path of weathering winds
Shall I worry it would rather turn from the fight
Will the storm let the hate of it dissolve it to dust
Shall it pull and hide it in the sand
What if I open my limbs, open wide and long
Will it put at bay the ripping bitterness
Storm winds have blown into the harbor with me
Will the fury of this storm break me at my base
Am I with age and at the point of brittleness
Are the northern winds pushing the rapids meant to wash me to sea
Or am and forever will I be
Someone's picture of beauty of this harbor beach

Patty Victory
Santa Barbara, CA

Our Friendship

As our todays become yesterdays and our lives proceed on their paths, directions and outcomes unknown, just knowing you are my friend comforts me during despair, makes me feel special for no reason, and it gives me a sense of security and belonging that affords me the strength to face and overcome life's obstacles and dilemmas.

My heart is forever touched as I think of all the things you have done for my benefit and advancement. Words of encouragement so warmly expressed, time and energy spent selflessly, and advice spoken with love and concern. I know that I am not the only person in your life, but you manage to make me feel as though I am at times.

Your life, your character, your heart and soul, they inspire me in so many regards. I strive to be more generous because you are so giving. I strive to be more understanding because you are so compassionate. I strive to be more diligent because you are so driven, and I strive to be a better person because you deserve that in a friend, and I want you to have a friend as wonderful as you.

Julie Christopher
Paris, KY

Two Sisters Plot

Being here has done no good, I've done all I can
But it takes more strength than what I've got
To make people understand
They don't know who I am, why do they judge me so?
It's because I'm different and they're all the same
And they're blind to what they don't know
I am who I am, to them that's nothing
Bring my world down again
One day, today, I'll be gone soon
But behind I'll leave my pain
Forfeit this war and slay yourself, no tears of mine shall fall
Let your hate unfold on me and complete yourself once and for all
Lay me down and bleed my veins, take my life from me
But be sure to leave me just a sip of my own agony
I hate you for who you are and I'll hate you 'til I die
Just one thing I'd like to ask and that is the question—why?
What did I do to you to rip your feelings raw?
Maybe one day, in your mind, you can see the things I saw
Whispering hate without a source
Contained silence that will ache
You never know how bad it hurts until you finally break
I'm so unimportant to you, yet I'm your self-esteem toy
Someone so much lower than you for your simple words to destroy
Someone to make you feel good about yourself
When you've nothing better to do
But ya know, if I could have one wish, it would be the death of you

Christy Lanese Cryer
Merryville, LA

My Youth

In my youth I was strong
I had many promises
Now in my later years I am battered
Now let me live out my days in peace

James M. Tate
Independence, MO

No One Told Me

Today, no one told me that a person could die
within weeks, even days, because of this disease.
No one told me that a call in the night might be
the last that I would hear from them.
Tomorrow, I learn that a person I once knew and
loved is gone because of this disease.
What am I able to do?
Once told, I could not want more (sobriety) for a person
than what they want.
Today, no one told me, but with each person I have met,
I have made it a journey, like recovery
can be for a person because of this disease,
gratitude and life.

Faith Wilson
Granville, OH

The Class

In memory of our departed brothers and sisters

There once was a class that
Attended Atwood High.
They never met a stranger
They wouldn't give a big high-five.

They had a lot of happy days.
They also had some sad,
But trying to remember a sad one
Would almost drive you mad!

They played hard, they worked hard.
They labored and they toiled.
Some might like to say
They were just a little spoiled.

But being from the class
Of nineteen fifty-nine,
We will always be the best
Of all past and future time.

Andy Anderson
Alma, NE

Fall Came by Today

Fall came back to town today
She marched right back in her usual way.
The winds were gently blowing cool
The leaves fell off branches into the pool.
The squirrels were racing round and round
Looking for the acorns on the ground.
The leaves were turning orange, yellow, and red
They liked this better than green instead.
Soon all the colorful leaves were on the ground
I guess it's time for the rake to be found.
The days grow shorter and the nights grow longer
Every day the winds blow a little bit stronger.
I asked Fall if she'd like to stay
"I'm sorry, my dear, Winter's on his way."
So I guess I'll just have to enjoy her short visit
I'll frolic in her colorful apparel so I won't miss it.

Gail Korndoerfer
Browns Mills, NJ

Letter to My First Love

When I was still green and had blonde highlights
and relied on my mother for transportation,
I was delivered to your house
where we watched Disney's *Aladdin* in your basement
You gave me your Billy Joel tour shirt
and asked if you may kiss me
I watched your rugby games in the crisp autumn air
I always wore your team sweatshirt
I explained the game to the parents on the sidelines
You were easy to spot with your long curly hair
You came to my rugby matches
though your broad shoulders would not fit in my sweatshirt
We dressed up and went to dances
We dressed down and cooked frozen pizzas
You were meticulous about the placement of the pepperoni
For Christmas, you gave me a diamond ring
I wore it on my left hand
You have since left me
for different, perhaps better, things
It has been years
yet I still find my left hand bearing that ring
It only fits on that finger
None has ever filled your place
within my heart; I would still let you kiss me
and I, I would kiss back

Kittie Puhek
West Allis, WI

Life

I was born a son to my mother and dad.
A future president they knew they just had.
Four sons and a daughter, our family was poor.
Food and clothes we had, but wanted much more.
Neighborhood children for Christmas got bikes that were neat.
Our gifts were made with love and could not be beat.
Years went by and time went so fast.
Our family under one roof, I knew it would not last.
The oldest, to college he went with a smile on his face
In hopes in four years to join the rat race.
The next joined the army and to Vietnam he went
In hopes of bringing freedom to people he never met.
My parents were proud, they told him quite often.
Nine months later, he came home in a coffin.
The third son grew up in the turbulent sixties.
With long hair and full beard, he looked like the hippies.
Drugs he got into, to watch was so sad.
An overdose took him from me, no future he had.
My sister was next, she left me alone.
She met a good man to start their own home.
The time had come for me to leave the nest.
Off to college I went to do my best.
I met a young lady, my heart she did steal.
This had to be love because it felt so real.
Two years later, a son was born to his mother and me.
A future president we wanted, we will wait and see.

Dave Popejoy
Lucerne, IN

Our Lives

Life should be full of joy
Laughter and love
Death should be peaceful
Like Heaven above.
Fear should be hidden
Left to subside
While smiles replace
The tears we've cried.
Love should be healthy
Shared with others
Peace should be passed on
Through all, even sisters and brothers.
The world should be willing
To give and not take
To ignore selfish feelings
For everyone's sake.
Stand happy and bold
Refuse to be shy
Love should rule
War should die.
If people would listen
See what life's worth
The only thing left
Would be peace on Earth.

Dolores D. Wishon
New Cumberland, WV

I am happily married to Frank L. Wishon. We have three beautiful children, oldest son Robert W. Wishon, daughter Jessica M. Wishon, and youngest son, Cody W. Wishon. I write poetry to express my feelings and emotions. Growing up with a strong-minded mother and four sisters also gave me inspiration.

My Mom, a Superstar

My role model, my idol because that's what you are
A true champion survivor of a lot of bad times, my mom, a superstar
Putting up with a lot of s*** that you never deserved to put up with
I've always wondered how and why you've managed to handle it
I've always kept you right here up front in my face
'cause you were no joke, always leaving a lasting impression on me when
you opened up your mouth and spoke
See, I could laugh about all those ass-whoopings now,
but they damn sure weren't funny then
You've instilled good morals and values in me
To thank you, where would I begin?
I remember the time when you made me laugh
when deep down I wanted to cry, or how about the time when you gave
me that look when you knew I was telling a lie,
or how about this—at seventeen, thinking I knew it
and that I was grown, you gave me that tough love speech I
remember— saying, "Wait till you have kids of your own"—now I have
three
I have a good job and I'm almost in my prime
Boy, I say to myself, if I had that one wish, it would be
to turn back the hands of time because your grandchildren are
beautiful little pains in the butt—but one of them,
you never really knew, but when I look into her eyes
and I see her smile, it's your spirit that I see shine through
So I'm going to take things a little slower now and move at my pace
and stop all the riffin' and the fussin'
because this spiritual award that I present to you, Mom,
is definitely not open for discussion
So whether I'm reading a book or doing some laundry
or just riding around in my car, I'll always remember the one who
raised me to the best of her ability—my mom, a superstar.

Angela Gold
Brooklyn, NY

What Is Love?

Love is not an errand.
Love is not a chore.
Love is what you do
When you can't be away
From someone anymore.

Kira Stowell
Vancouver, WA

Life Has Too Much Pressure

A bunch of kids come from a broken home
Eighteen years old, now you're feeling so grown
No pops, moms trippin', now the stress keeps growing
The world goes at a fast pace
So the life you live is not slowin'
Each day as a person we keep growin'
And try to stay ahead of the pressure
It may take time, but I'm starting to realize
I'm starting to realize my life I should treasure
Like a bird with its feathers, life after death
I will fly high
Heaven, where everybody up top is kind
Good dreams got me feelin' good signs

Steven Goode
Inglewood, CA

I Am

I am a carefree girl who loves rabbits.
I wonder if there is a rabbit that can fly.
I hear the rabbits chewing corn.
I see a rabbit with golden wings soaring over the water.
I want it to fly safely over the water.
I am a carefree girl who loves rabbits.

I pretend that rabbits can talk.
I feel they understand me.
I touch the clouds on a winged rabbit.
I worry that my rabbits will be killed by a crazed killer.
I cry when my rabbits die.
I am a carefree girl who loves rabbits.

I understand that rabbits can't fly.
I say one day maybe they might.
I dream of traveling to Alabama in the summer
With my rabbits.
I try to be the best trainer I can be.
I hope to train rabbits all my life.
I am a carefree girl who loves rabbits.

Lanaya Warner
Portsmouth, OH

I'm Lanaya Warner. I live with my parents, John and Martha Warner. I have three sisters, all married: Lajohna Campbell, Lori Yarnell, and Lisa Williams. I have three nieces: Stormy and Holly Williams and Caitlin Fannin. My teacher, Mrs. Susie Wayne, at the Scioto Country Joint Vocational School, where I graduated, got me interested in poetry. She had her own notebook that she kept the best poems in. Mine was one of them. I was inspired to write this poem because my mom and I raise and show Californian mini-Rex and mini-satin rabbits. We show all over Ohio. We have sixty-five rabbits.

A Mother's Goodbye

At last I'm home in Heaven
Safely in God's hands,
The joy and beauty of this place
Is more than I can stand.
My pain and grief are over
No more sleepless nights.
Now I'll rest forever
In this everlasting light.
I've done my best for what it's worth
To guide you on your way,
It's time for you to stand up tall
And try not to go astray.
Although I'll miss you dearly
I truly have to say,
I took God's hand willingly
And really want to stay.
Please don't cry or grieve for me
Please know that I am fine,
And know that I will always love you
'Til the end of time.
I know we'll be together again
Someday much later in time,
Until I see you in God's arms
Be good, stay safe, be kind.

Michele Fontana
Bear, DE

It was just a couple of months after my father died that I decided I wanted to have something personal put on the back of my prayer card when I die for my children to keep. I raised my four children by myself and we have a very strong bond between us. I love my children more than anything in this world, and we are all very close. I needed to reassure them that when I die, they must go on and just remember the love that we had and stay a close-knit family. Hopefully this poem will accomplish that.

Hello, Stranger

The day I saw you get off the bus
I knew from that moment, it was a must
You were handsome, sexy, and mine
I knew it was only a matter of time
Before we would never want to part
From that moment, it was our start
We connected on so many things
That I knew it was because of angel's wings
I didn't believe in faith or fate
But I was shown how to not hate
We had our disagreements at first
But we got through the worst
Then we got married for my mom
And your brother-in-law calls you Tom
Then we moved to the east
Oh, what a fun and exciting feast
I got to meet your mom and dad
Wow, I wish my mom wasn't so sad
Your brother and sisters are fun
At first, I was stunned
About how loving and kind they were
I though we would cause a stir
But here we are after a year
And I'm still so happy without a tear.

Patricia Nealon
Hagerstown, MD

I Would

If you asked me to calm the day
I would
To make a cloud from reddened clay
I would
Ask me to craft a poem from the wind
And the stormy night
To stir you threaded daydreams from the
Heaven's light
I would
There is but one thing that for you
I could not do
I could not die for you
Not die
No, not for you
I would
Calm the day and
Make a cloud and
Craft a poem and
Stir your heart
But
I could not die for you
Because
I already do.

Courtney Marti
Rosemount, MN

Living a Smile

I sat to write of love and woes
Never able to end it . . .
When suddenly a thought arose
Maybe writing of the future and not the past would be a better fit!
Suffering and heartbreak is very real
And surrounds us on a daily basis.
We all know the pain of having to heal;
Why not describe a different end to these races?
Change for goodness and open wide minds,
Communication, togetherness, broadening your horizon;
Taking the lesser traveled, not the straight,
But the road that winds,
Showing your fears, what gives you pause, why your heart weighs a ton.
Knowing that even if the one you chose
Leaves you alone, high and dry,
You're better for it, as the story goes,
That cliche is not a lie!
Being honest and living outside of vicious denial
Caring for others for which you profess your love . . . or not,
Opening our hearts and minds, living a smile,
Giving everything always the tip-top most you have got.

Margaret Stirewalt
Salisbury, NC

A Life Alone

A life alone—it isn't so bad.
A life alone—there's much to be had.
A life alone—what a life to lead!
A life alone—no one to heed.
A life alone—on a solitary beach.
A life alone—the wave can't even reach.
A life alone—a salesman's dream.
A life alone is not what it seems!
A life alone can be a very grand thing.
In a life alone, there's nothing to bring.
A life alone leaves no chance to fall,
But a life utterly alone is no life at all.

A week alone breeds such thoughts.
A week alone is hard and wrought.
A week alone drove me nuts.
A week alone filled with buts.
A day not alone was all I could ask,
A life alone became my task.
A life alone works for so many,
But to me, a life alone is not worth a penny.

Franklin E. Morgan
Eagle Springs, NC

Freedom

Freedom is red, white, and blue.
It sounds like a magnificent trumpet.
It tastes like a well-rounded apple, sweet and sour.
It smells like a wonderfully cooked loaf of bread.
Freedom feels great like a big storm passing into
The freedom of the blue sky.

Noah Gunnink
Delawan, WI

The thing I like about poetry is when you write and write, it flows out of you. What inspired me was when we made a book of poetry in language arts. That was really it. I would like to dedicate this poem to all the soldiers who fought for our country so we can have freedom. I am in the seventh grade and I am twelve years old. I love to hunt, fish, bowl, shoot trap, and now poetry. Please enjoy my poem and remember all who fought for your freedom. God bless!

The Breakup

Today is the day
I'm going to sail away
I've been a poor recluse
But now I'm bustin' loose
Sorry I have to go
Can't take this stuff no mo'
Today I will try
To make myself not cry
I'm tired of being hurt
You make me feel like dirt
I'm the best you've ever had
So why are you so mad
You tried to be my boss
And now you'll pay the cost
I'm leaving, won't be back
Today I'll start to pack
Tomorrow I'll be gone
And you'll be all alone
You'll ask me to stay
And I will say "No way"
My mind says "I can't take it"
But you say "We can make it"
Little do you know
This is the final show
I'm leaving you today
I'm going far away

Sarah Womack
Greensboro, NC

Sadness, Interrupted

When I look in a mirror all I see are sad eyes
Eyes all red from pain and anger
Life has to move on no more feeling hopeless and alone
I can only see the pain I so want to end
Not knowing what lays underneath
All I see is tears in those eyes
Wanting the hole in my heart to quickly heal
My head and heart are still in the dark
Wanting and waiting to be seen in the light
Wishing my anger to melt away
There has to be room for joy in my eyes
From all this I see my strength pulling me in to the light
Where there is hope that comes shining through

Leslie V. Lynde
Parsippany, NJ

Roses and a Little Girl

Have you taken time to "smell the roses"?
Well, if not, for shame, for shame.
A little girl spoke to her family and then over she came.
For a special occasion, my husband was holding a red rose bouquet.
She asked if she could smell them and my husband said, "Okay."

"Would you like to hold them for a while?"
She said "Thank you" and took them, giving him a great big smile.
She poked her little nose into the bunch
And then crinkled up her nose.
With a puzzled look on her face, she again smelled the rose.

She said, "You know, they're really pretty,
But they don't have any smell.
The ones we grow at home are 'smelly' and are also pretty as well."
She thanked my husband and then she skipped away.
That little girl had wisdom, wouldn't you say?

Home-grown things are usually the best
Because they stand out from all the rest.
Take time to "smell the roses" wherever they are found,
It will bring a smile to your face and maybe turn your day around!

Carol Spear
Hilliard, FL

Impression, the Internal Expressionist

Faded in a mystic hue
Of blue and green,
Human forms painted.
One with a body in twist.
A schism, an impenetrable shist.
From the painting
Her backside stares at me.
Inviting, in a calm,
Withdrawn position.
Yet of the four
Painted here, I envision
A mixture, a montage,
A depiction of them all.
I turn to relish the impression,
The internalized expression,
And it paints a subliminal picture
Distinguished, in a mystic hue
Of blue and green
Upon the backdrop
Of a womanless scene.

Gary Oram
Dillon, MT

Gary Oram Jr. writes the sports page at the *Dillow Tribune* in the Big Sky country of Montana. In the fall of 2010, he will be a senior at the University of Montana Western, working toward an arts/English degree in creative writing. He is an avid author who has completed several novels, novellas, and epic poems. At present, he is writing an epic science fiction, involving the formation of known space and the formation of the unknown. He enjoys horseback riding, reading a good novel, and never having missed a deadline.

Lady Justice

Lady Justice, where are you? Your children are calling.
The world is in turmoil, and nations are falling.

You're not seen in the eyes of those ravaged by war,
or the homeless and hungry that abound shore to shore.

You're not seen in the eyes of the child so abused,
or the innocent man who stands wrongly accused.

Where are you, dear lady? Are you too blind to see
that the world and your children are no longer free?

Cast off your blindfold, and wield your sword high.
Give us some hope, or we surely shall die.

Save us, dear lady, from our ominous fate.
Oh, save us, dear lady, before it's too late.

Lois E. Van Mun
Kooskia, ID

You and Me

You tell me you love me
And I tell you the same.
However, the meaning of trust
Seems to be our favorite game.

Life is short, and life is sweet.
There is just not enough time to always
Feel the need to over-speculate!

I trust you, just as you should me.
Neither of us is never alone,
Only because we both work as a team.

I have no reason to ever lie to you,
Just as you yourself never lie to me.
I wish I was like you,
So strong and ever so bold!

I know I am far from perfect,
And I probably never will be,
So all I can ask of you
Is to love me for me!

Melissa Prescott
Riverside, MO

Wife

This is the girl I call wife—
She is a special lady,
She is the joy of my life.
I don't just mean maybe.
This is the girl they call Mother—
She is a very special lady
And there is no other,
And they don't mean maybe.
There is this girl they call friend
For she is some kind of lady.
She will be loved through the end
That's not just maybe.
This is the girl patient
She is a durable lady
She seems awful hesitant
There is no maybe.
This is the girl I call daughter—
She is a proven lady.
I often see her at the altar;
She is going to be with me,
And that's no maybe.

Earl Hardy
Oil City, LA

I was born on March 16, 1940 in Many, Louisiana to godly parents. I am the sixth in a family of seven children, the youngest of a set of twins. I enjoyed reading poetry as a child in grade school, but never thought of writing poetry until February 1999 when my wife was in the hospital, just before she passed away. Seeing her in her condition inspired me to write of her. I realize it pertains to the way some other men feel about their wives. May this poem inspire other people to have a greater love for their companions. I am thankful for the opportunity to have this poem published.

The Coward

I'd like to run away someday
Away from all I know
But alas, I am a coward
And I'll do as I'm told
I'd like to break free
From the grasp of higher authorities
And shake my fist at them
And stand up for my beliefs
But alas, I am a coward
I should like to fly
Up in the air, alone
Nothing to hold me down
No one to answer to
But alas, I am a coward
I want out of this dungeon
It's dark and damp and cold
But alas, I am a coward
And can't find my way home
I'd like to tell you what I think
But you might not agree
I'd like to tell you how I feel
But alas, I am a coward
I'd like to do all these things
And perhaps someday I shall
I'd like to do them all today
But alas, I am a coward

Kiah Beeman
FPO, AP

I am fourteen years old, and I attend Lester Middle School in Okinawa, Japan. I wrote this poem about people who want to say something but are too afraid of retaliation to stand up for their beliefs. It was written for my creative writing portfolio for school. I am honored to be included in this publication and hope that you enjoy my poetry. I would like to thank these people for supporting me and my poetry: Faith, Lisa, and Michael Beeman; Ronald Coia, English teacher; the Desjardins; and Michelle Watson, creative writing teacher.

You Can't Go Home Again

You can't go home again
To earth and field and flowers,
Or stroll along the babbling brook
And while away the hours.

You can't go home again
To friends and kindred rare,
For time has scattered them afar
And they are no longer there.

You can't go home again
To scenes of childhood play,
For many passings of the sun
Have hidden them away.

You can't go home again
To magnolia-covered lawn,
For those who made that place a home
Are now long since gone.

Fred W. Holdsworth
Rocky Mount, NC

Dad

I hug your lifeless body goodbye for now.
As your soul flies out of my reach, I cry.
Now I'm an open book.
My friends see how I feel from the look on my face.
My head drops.
I cry in fear of what I may become, but I try to stay strong.
I talk like nothing has happened, but I'm behind locked doors.
I'm waiting for something.
I don't know why or what I'm waiting for.
My heart is shielded. My feelings are twisted and confused.
I don't know what to do.
My mind is filled with anger.
My eyes are pouring out tears.
My heart is broken.
My mind is made up, I have to move on.
I lost my father January eighteenth, two thousand and ten,
I look and look, but I can't find any remains.
Songs and movies remind me of you, bring tears to my eyes and hurt to
my heart.
I miss you dearly and I will all the way up to the day I die.
When will that day come, when will you, my mother, and I be
reunited?

Crystal Rose Mosher
Cedar Rapids, IA

What Is a Mother?

What is a mother?
Does anyone really know?
To endure the pain of childbirth
And then to love us so.

What is a mother?
Can anyone every say?
To willingly sacrifice her life
For her child every day.

She helps us battle our little fears
And gently guides us through the years,
And when she's done her very best,
She reluctantly helps us leave the nest.

And even as we age,
And depend on Mom no more,
We're always drawn back to her
Like a ship drawn back to shore.

So how does one define the word,
The word that's like no other,
The word we've known from childhood,
The word we know as "mother"?

Howard J. Bennett
Mexico, NY

You and Me

You were young
And I was young
And life eternity
The day we chose
To share it all
Between us,
You and me.
Time moves on,
Life goes along,
And every day we see
A love sealed
Everlasting bond
Between us,
You and me.
And through
The years to come,
We know that there
Will always be
A love that's young
And beautiful
Between us,
You and me.

Carol W. Allen
Big Pine Key, FL

Pain

Pain, oh, precious pain,
How I live with you!
You are everywhere
I do not want you to be.
Pain, oh, precious pain.
Sometimes you are so strong
You could kill me
And sometimes I wish you would.
Pain, oh, precious pain.
You are so cruel and hurtful!
You cause me so much hurt
I think of hurting myself.
Pain, oh, precious pain.
Why do you haunt me?
You follow me like a shadow.
Do you know how much you hurt me?
Pain, oh, precious pain,
Please go away and leave me alone.
I hate you!
Pleasc go bother someone else.
Pain, oh, precious pain.
You caused me to hate people
I should care about and love
But you will not release me.

Anne Martin
Hamlet, NC

Mr. Tree and Me

I am the tree and imitation of life
I exude oxygen and shade though with mankind I'm at strife
I stand tall and bold in the heat and in the cold
The nature of the beast eradicates my soul
They chop and disfigure my very essence
It seems as no one appreciates my presence
Beautiful and courageous also rooted and strong
Vicariously me and the tree have the same thing going on.

Emmanuel Scott
Hickory, NC

Stress

Fingernails bitten
cuticles receding
skin broken and bleeding
stress
grinds
down
like the weight of the world
resting on my shoulders.
I wonder if this is how
the Titan Atlas felt
when Zeus placed the sky
upon his back.

Crystal Ice
Romeoville, IL

The Ultimate Solution

As God looks down from Heaven
surveying His Master plan,
He thinks that of all His creatures,
He never could fathom Man.

"Who is more the righteous?"
"Who will last the longer?"
God becomes impatient with,
"Just who'll become the stronger?"

Wearily God watches
this morbid evolution,
knowing Man could annihilate
with its "ultimate solution."

For it's truly a contradiction
when it's seen so definitely
that the height of Man's intelligence
should prove the depth of Man's stupidity.

Ilse Roberts
Newnan, GA

Memorial Day 2001

Holiday weekends are the blue patch in a rain-filled sky.
Even when the rain pours inside,
it cools and fills the soul.
Freedom tastes glorious as forgotten fragrances fill the air;
could that be fatback sizzling on the grill?
I smell the memories of family reunions
at Willie Brackett's house in Sapulpa, Oklahoma
when we were all together in the 1960s.

But we weren't all together in the 1960s.
America lost its bearings in that psychedelic fog;
Beat Generation morphed into flower children
whose petals were scattered over southeast Asia.

"But the devil made me do it!" Right, Mr. President!
The iron grip of popularity poisoned your mind,
so you flew too near the sun and scrambled your brain.
We tuned in and dropped out,
    our naked souls too fragile
    to withstand *la verite*.

We lost our legs before we ever started the race,
like bells always singing off-key, into infinity.
"God helps those who help themselves"; we help ourselves
    to everything on Earth; therefore, we are—
    God!
Gathering clouds thicken, distorting these images,
even as exploding memories flame into and sear the future.

Kitty Bradley
Monrovia, MD

Enlightenment

True life is not about us, now what we want, not what we need,
not what we think, nor what we see.
It's about others, the ones we know,
the ones we don't and the ones who simply won't.
Life's about how we can help, how we can share
and how we can always be there.
Life is a gift from the One above
by allowing us an opportunity to love,
choosing grace over sorrow and enlightenment for the morrow.

Thomas Hatley
Bolingbrook, IL

Always and Forever

They say age is a number, a total
of all the years,
a summary of the laughter, sadness, and tears,
but what about the heart, does it go
on feeling passion?
Can it still feel ecstasy?
Could there be a true love for you and me?
If a person comes into your life, gives
you happiness beyond belief, what matters
what the numbers are?
Enjoy every moment, yours to keep.

Eileen Barwick
Smallwood, NY

A Cowboy's Farewell to His Horse

You've helped me cut a maverick
And bring him to the brand
You've helped me rope a dogie
A-squealin' in the sand,
But now when things look very dark
And death is near at hand
You'll still a-help me ropin'
In another kind of land.

When it is dark and cold and still
And weary life is o'er,
You'll feel at last your freedom
As I loose your hackamore.
You'll go a-thund'ring out the gate,
The bond of life has tore,
But still I'll hear your clatt'ring hoofs
Resound the canyon floor.

Joan C. Wood
Hartsdale, NY

My Calling

The wind of night was blowing
upon a hill so steep.
I heard a voice start calling
as I slumbered oh, so deep.

I awoke again that morning
and looked around my bed.
I saw the Earth below me
and a ring around my head.

Claire Dal Corso
Costa Mesa, CA

Nightclubs

The drinking and dancing
the sound of hollow laughter.
What in the world
are these people doing?
What are they searching after?

Talking loud and dressed to kill
out trying to impress.
I suppose they are unsure inside
and suffer loneliness.

Lois Cherry
Hubbardston, MA

Recipe for Homemade Love

Add two cups of homemade love
Sent from God above.
Mix together a tablespoon of honesty,
A tablespoon of generosity.
Stir in half a cup of devotion,
Sprinkle in a dash of emotion.
Pray to the Lord day by day,
Add some faith and hope along the way.
Melt together one cup of hugs and kisses,
Add a pinch of warm wishes.
Blend in one cup of happiness,
Add two cups of tenderness.
Then add a dash of sunshine
From your heart to mine.
For the sad years,
Mix in a bottle of our tears.
Shake in one full cup of laughter
For now and ever after.
Add a dash of time,
Things will work out fine.
Mix until well blended,
Now this love recipe had ended.
Just bake at thirty degrees for one loving hour,
Along with God's almighty power.

PS—this recipe, use again and again.
Amen.

Jennifer J. Johnson
Bay City, MI

Untitled

It's autumn and the leaves are dry
And rustle on the ground as chilly winds go whistling by
With low and pensive sounds as in the graveyard
I slowly creep with meditation's lead
I walked with slow and cautious feet above the sleeping dead
There three little graves range side by side
It's there my close attention grew—
For over the tall grass bending side
There one seemed fresh and new
I said, Mother, you told me if I would not cry
You would show me where sweet sister lies
It's here, my child, sweet sister lies deep
Buried in the ground
No light comes to her little eyes, nor she can hear no sound
Mother, can't we dig sweet sister up
I'll put her in my little bed
I'll fed her from my little cup and there she won't be dead
No, my child, that will never do
For God, whom saw her die as He looked down from Heaven
And smiled and called her to the sky
Her body in the grave is dead
But sister lives in Heaven

Ann Brewer
Spirit Lake, ID

Retired

So you're retired, but can't relax
I know something to fix just that
There's nothing better than a fishing trip
Something that won't make you sick

All you need is fishing gear, a chair to sit on
And something to drink
You can take a lunch, but no time to eat
So sit down, my friend, you'll be relaxed
I told you my remedy works

The rods and reels are getting old
Worth more to us than all the gold
They're still fine, yours and mine
We'll go again a few more times
So keep relaxed, give a big smile
You know my remedy was well worthwhile

Katheryn Wagner
Algood, TN

Untitled

So many words never spoken
So many things left undone
Life is what it is, can't change
What's been, but we can always
Hope for a better tomorrow

Alicia Alberto
Foster City, CA

Mama

So often I find myself thinking of you
and longing to see your face.

To talk to you about life,
to feel your gentle hand upon my fevered brow.

To hear your laughter and to hear you sing "Three little fishes,"
but that cannot be for now.

As God has called you home to be with Him,
Someday I shall be there too.

Until then, I'll keep you in my heart.
I love you, Mama!

Kathy Paschal
Salt Lake City, UT

April's Child

I think of you when lilacs bloom
And fragrant sentries guard my room
Against the pall of winter's gloom
And beckon spring with sweet perfume.
I think of you when lilacs bloom.
I think of you when violets dot
The borders of my garden plot
A quiet treasure to be sought.
I think of you when violets dot
The borders of my garden plot.
Please think of me as leaves unfold
And later as they turn to gold.
We've gathered all our arms will hold
My memory's gone and you are old
Please think of me as leaves unfold.

Joan Kathleen Swartz Clellan
Galloway, OH

This poem, written for my father's birthday in April, memorializes our shared love for poetry, flowers, and the magic of the growing season. Both privileged to be born and reared on a family farm in northwestern Ohio, my father and I often roamed our woods where I absorbed his fascinating teachings about plants, flowers, and trees. After graduating summa cum laude from the Ohio State University with a comprehensive English major and earning a law degree, I pursued my law practice. Later, I began writing gospel music and singing; however, the soft, subtle art of poetry is my truest passion.

In Commemoration of All Great Cities All Over the United States

Always moving,
moving, moving
I can feel
your vibrations.
Your heartbeat
is thumping, thumping
and swaying in unison,
with overflowing
coffee.
Everywhere there
is a vision.
Everywhere people
in a huff.

You are full
and alive.
I can almost hear
the sounds of typewriters and
ticker tapes
clicking, clicking . . .
business booming . . .
the vibrations
of endless life.

Lesley J. Sagel
Philadelphia, PA

Our Children

Children are gifts from our dear Lord above,
Those who receive them must give them their love.

We feed them, we clothe them, we send them to school,
Praying that no one treats them unfairly or cruel.

We teach them good morals, what's fair and what's right,
Never cheat, never lie, and never start a fight.

If you try out for football, cheerleader, or dance,
Work very hard—don't leave it to chance.

But what if the teachers are cruel and unfair
And try to convince you that they truly care?

I know this sounds crazy, it couldn't be true
I just hope it doesn't happen to you!

Beverly Kelly Vacek
Palacios, TX

So Beautiful and Grand

I see them walking hand in hand
upon the seashore barefoot in the sand.
The love between them is so beautiful and grand.
I watch them as they stroll past me.
The gentle seashore breeze shuffles
through their salt and pepper hair.
They have no cares, just living in the moment,
making yet another memory to cherish between them.
My heart flutters with envy and awe,

leaving me wishing I could find a love as special as theirs.
They disappear into the distance
as a single tears falls from my face; I wipe it away
and turn and walk away,
hoping that someday I, too will find a love
so beautiful and grand as theirs.

Nancy R. Cash
Tyler, TX

Family Reunions

Whenever we celebrate and get together
we aren't there to discuss the weather.
We all have things we wish to say
about our lives now and yesterday.

Our togetherness today shows how we care
for all our family, whether here or there.
Pictures we bring and new additions are added
as new memories unfold and hearts are padded.

Family on Earth and family above
are with us now and share our love.
As God is with us to celebrate this day
more of His love will come our way.

Barbara A. Williams
Highland, NY

Going Hunting

Up early before the sun
All set to go with your big old gun.
No matter how cold,
Or if it snows,
For you are dressed in your goose-down clothes.
Sit up in a tree or in your truck.
Just hope to see a big old buck.
Does by the number will you probably see,
Now how far behind can that buck be?
And when he finally steps into view,
The sight on your gun is not true.
You shoot a little to the left
Or a little to the right . . .
No matter now,
He's out of sight!

Sandra H. Pilgreen
Tarboro, NC

Bea

My firstborn child, my little girl.
I love you more than anything in this world.
You are very special, you are my heart.
My love for you will never, ever part.
When I first saw you, my first
thought was, "My God, she's too beautiful to be mine,"
but there you were, so beautiful and small.
I was so proud and scared at the same time.
When I first saw you, the pain didn't feel so bad.
Laying there with your head full of black hair,
I couldn't wait to hold you to show you how much I care.
You were the first of three,
I kinda wish that more I would have had,
but never forget, no matter what life has in store,
that even if I tried, I couldn't love you more.
I'll always be here for you and your family.

Pauline Ramirez
Oneonta, AL

New York

People talk about New York, I dare
Though anywhere else, you'll find crime there.
It's such a beautiful place to be.
New York, New York, just come and see.

New York, New York, visitors come in throngs
To visit places they heard about.
Do come, my friend, don't be afraid
Because New York is a wonderful place.

Folks come in buses, planes, and trains
To visit New York, this wonderful place.
Come, my dear friend, come and sightsee,
Visit places like the Statue of Liberty.

There are beautiful tall buildings
You will adore.
When you visit New York City,
You won't be bored.

Ellis Island is one place you should see.
When you come to New York, you will agree.
Don't listen to what others say, come see for yourself,
It's such a beautiful place.

Urita S. Arthur
Brooklyn, NY

I am eighty-two years young and a mother of six children, eighteen grandchildren, and twenty-one great-grandchildren. I came to the United States of America forty years ago, and know this is a great country of ample opportunity. Poetry has been my lifelong dream because you can express yourself, the way you feel. Sometimes I write poetry and prayers and distribute them to friends. One day my youngest daughter said, Mom, why don't you publish a book, but I never really thought about it. I do have a few I kept for myself, and surely would love to publish some of them.

Guardian Angel

Be with me every waking hour
Of every precious day
Help me to do my work in life
And gain in every way

Be with me guardian angel sweet
When decisions I must make
Show me how to steady my feet
And the proper road to take

Take my hand and lead me
To righteous paths and truth
Give me the wisdom of ages
And the adventurous heart of youth

Help me remember the good things
That bind all in spirit toward One
Help me find the solution
To live with malice toward none

Be by me always dear angel
On whatever path I may trod
And then when my journeys are over
Lead me back home to my God

Maria E. Tuzzo
Jersey City, NJ

I Get Lonely

Sometime I can't speak the English,
that's why I'm deaf so lonely.
I walk to the open door, but the sound of
the rain on the roof of my car
makes me scared in the dark in my dream-sleep.
You see passenger side wearing that blue
scarf, I get you for our celebration.
That's where you sat when you said
to me, you think that space is what you need,
time to decide where you want to be. So now
every time that it rains, I get lonely.
I begin to miss your touch. I get lonely I start
to reminisce of us. I get lonely as it rains,
isn't sad enough.
Every time it starts to rain on me, I get
lonely.
You had a smile like summertime and hair
like a gentle breeze. A sudden change
in the weather.
Now you are no longer with me. You wanted space,
I gave the universe. You wanted time,
I gave eternity. Tears of the sky remind
of hurt. So now every time that it rains,
I get lonely. That's why I am deaf, so
lonely.

Michael King
Snellville, GA

My Dream Catcher

I saw you outside my window
swaying so soundly in the breeze,
catching my imagination with your pretty colors,
strings and turtle dove feathers.

Bells are ringing to the sounds
of my dreaming as I can't help but smile
as light floods in from the window.
This warmth is filling me up inside and I feel so alive.

Pretty piano notes playing,
matching the bells outside my window,
fleeting like the fickle dance of the feather
draping over its shoulder.

Watching you now I wonder to myself
why it is I let the little things get to me,
so I let them go,
becoming so light I could fly away.

Outside my window,
I watched you sway so soundly in the breeze
and thanked you kindly
for freeing me.

Jennifer Staysa
Castro Valley, CA

A Vegetarian Cannibal's Last Meal

I'd buy light years of rope
that's been blessed by the pope
for a sip!
I'd pull down the moon
so it's full until June
please, a drink!
I'd tell jokes until dawn
would you laugh or just yawn?
I try to help you with lots of things
traveled to Spain and became the king
Real proud of myself I got so tall
but a giant walked in and everyone saw
He assumed command and ordered the chef
She brought out the food, but he'd already left
No one said "Nay," they just laughed it off
I walked out once, got and earful of cough
I'd take slices of Pi
till the finish was nigh
They just ate
I'd float in the air
prove gravity isn't there
They looked down
but he comes inside
tells an elaborate lie
and they clap!

Jude Waguespack
Oxford, GA

Too Young

Being too young to remember the days
When he indulged in his boisterous ways.
Being a child with a flowery mind,
I did not perceive that he was falling behind.

Too soon, for he knew the time of his fate,
He sequentially developed a new personality trait.
One of fake visage and a deceiving role,
And the abuse of potions beyond his control.

I think now he realized he was in too deep,
He voiced numerous promises he could not keep.
A derived unbalance made him go away,
Oblivious to the quandary, I wished he would stay.

Being too young to know him as a son could do,
I sometimes dreamed that we would start anew.
Wondering about the affinity we should have had,
A yearning for guidance; I wish I knew my dad.

David Whitehead
Woodinville, WA

Bon Voyage

My hand is writing what my mind explores,
I travel to the places that I see.
I'm venturing to near and distant shores
where waves come forth in clear transcendency,
for what are waves but thoughts that ebb and flow
to touch upon the hourglass of sand.
I gather shells of treasures found aglow
while delving into ocean depths and land.
There's crying of the gulls in air, profound;
they rise up as the waves and face the wind.
My hand is writing, as in flight, I've found
new beach, untrodden places to begin
another grand excursion with my pen—
a place to go and write about again.

Lucia Kiersch Haase
Spring Valley, IL

Untitled

Soft spoken words, a vision that blurs,
Unkind tears and realistic fears,
Unknown foes along with abundant woes,
Allies surprise! Nothing but lies.
Much love to the one who tries.

Away in time, lost from truth,
Unaware of the beauty in youth.
Corrupted soul takes its toll,
Body aches as I grow cold.

The summer air remains forever fair,
The roses bloom without a care.
The bunnies play in their perfect way,
Lilies in the field so beautifully displayed.
How I wonder why we've strayed.

Prison bars and youth-begotten scars,
Dirty cells and the pressure that swells,
Fading dreams and distant screams,
But somehow I sense it isn't as bad as it seems.

Michael Lamartina
Baltimore, MD

Day of Today

Today the clouds came in so dark
and gray.
As it passes, the winds begin to gust
away.
You could hear the leaves on the trees
blow to the east
like a roaring sound of a beast.

Today the sun came to light, slightly
so bright.
As it brought a cold chill, a whistle
sound blew and everything stood still.

Today is now night, and tomorrow
will come to show its own light.
As today comes to an end,
we anticipate the wait of tomorrow
as it soon shall be a . . .

day of today.

Diana L. Baca
Buena Park, CA

The Rain

The sun sets and rises.
It's another numb day,
A day of pushing forward.
My apartment is the same.
My friends are the same,
But I remember the rain.
It lasted many hectic days
As I uncovered Internet's secrets.
After seventeen lovely years,
He was looking for other women.
I terminated the relationship
Without a confrontation.
'Mid the ritual of daily activities,
Sometimes in trancelike moods,
I move through another day—
And I still remember the rain.

Mildred Pelkey
Glen Burnie, MD

New Orleans

Cultural gateway to North America,
Queen City of the south,
Birthplace of jazz,
Home of Mardi Gras;
Enchanting, indulgent, partying,
The Big Easy.
You are a city of crime; your stabbings, shootings, and robberies
are reported nightly.
You are a city of poverty; your poor can be seen in many of your
neighborhoods as one drives by.
You are a city of devastation; you suffered a loss because of Katrina that
affected the entire country.
I say to you there is crime in every city; the bigger the city, the more
crime there is.
National Guard members that patrolled your streets have now joined
your police force to help make you safer.
You are the city that care forgot. Your people have pulled together to
rebuild,
renew,
rebirth.
Their roots are as deep as the Mississippi and their blood bleeds purple,
green, and gold.
Jazz is playing,
nightlife is kicking,
everyone wants to party or second line!

Dottie May Paulson
New Orleans, LA

Through a Grave-Tinted Eye

I look out on the world through a grave-tinted eye
With phantom vultures soaring high
When summer's grip is broken and winter's chill draws nigh
Leaves drift from the trees waving a last forlorn goodbye
Rattling together like bones old and dry
Tossed hither and yon by the wind's low mournful sigh
Brilliant red flames against a gloomy grey sky
The tears of another year as it crawls away to die.

Joseph Ruble
McLeansville, NC

Dad

Sittin' in my room being sad.
Laying on my bed, thinking of my dad.
No matter how many times I toss and turn in this bed,
Just the image of his face going through my head.
I know he's watching over me every day.
Just the image in my head, it won't go away.
Thought I got signs of lightning and thunder
Knowing that my dad is six feet under.
I think in my head, should I blame myself?
I just close my eyes, trying to think of something else.
I lay on my back and look up at the sky,
Just keep asking myself, why?

Chelsea Kilgore
New Carlisle, OH

Let Freedom Ring

Lord, we recall that fateful day
When terror struck our land.
We're thankful You united us,
And helped us take a stand!

With humble hearts we come to You,
Unworthy though we be.
We pray You would show us the way
To keep this great land free!

Americans lend helping hands
Wherever there's a need.
They bond together for a cause,
Determined to succeed!

America's a freedom land,
Where hopes and dreams come true.
Lord, though we thank You not enough,
We owe it all to You!

May our Statue of Liberty,
With freedom torch held high,
Remain a symbol of our hope
For peace as time goes by!

Please spare us from the misery
That terrorists might bring.
Help us keep Old Glory flying,
Dear God, let freedom ring!

Elaine Kestly
Manitowoc, WI

Nightmare to a Dream

In the beginning his hands were warm,
and ever so soft to the touch.
His mere presence was such an awesome rush.
Suddenly and what seemed like overnight,
I was now three months pregnant.
He created my whole world full of
despair and sheer fright.
This man once appearing a tower of strength,
now appeared to be a demon sent
to hurt and destroy me, my self-esteem.
What a paradox and truly hard to believe.
From him, the nightmare,
my beautiful baby boy was conceived.
A devotion to faith and things unseen,
because God can always make a nightmare into a dream.

Kimberly Canada
Centreville, VA

Homecoming

I salute
The soldier
Came home
In the flag-wrapped box
From Afghanistan
I saw
Beside him
The uniformed brothers
Carry the box
While the trumpet plays
The sun shines
The tears dry!
I heard
The soldier whisper
I am home
Baby

Ngoc Thuy Nguyen
Riverside, CA

A Part of Me

You have been a dream that walked,
And held me by the hand and talked.
You have been a voice that stilled,
All yearnings so long unfilled.
You have been a fire that came
Into my heart with a sudden flame.
You have been the sun by day,
A star at night that led the way.
Music, laughter, moon aglow,
A kiss too long, too deep to go.
As life brought us together as one,
We shared life's joys and fun,
And when there comes a time of sadness,
Our love shared will bring us gladness.
Then once again the stars will shine,
As always and forever you are mine,
You have been and will ever be
A vital, breathing part of me.

Lynn D. Goddard
Rocky Point, NC

I am the daughter of two very creative parents—one an artist and one a fashion designer. My grandmother and I loved gardening and flowers, and thus, when I grew up, I became a floral designer. I started writing poetry in my late teens and continued to do so most of my life. When my husband became ill with cancer, I wanted to write a special poem for him—it meant a lot to him. I lost him in 1985. To this day and always, he is "A Part of Me."

Planet on Fire

Dissolving glaciers—
Animals fighting for their lives
Atmospheric smoke
Choking, when inhaled, a fright
Freezing and heating temperatures galore—
Is this what this planet was really made for?
Flooding waters—
People having no place to live
A planet raging on fire,
Something has to give
We are a planet of hope, and not despair
So come on, people, let's show how we care
We all can save this planet of ours
We are even smart enough to go to Mars
If we do not want this planet to die
It's not just for looking for answers in the sky
The answers lie in us all
We cannot let this planet fall

Marilyn J. Blattner
McKinney, TX

Monarch Butterfly

It's spring again
Bright orange and black
Returning from Mexico and California
Looking for milkweed plants
Each lay seven hundred eggs
Caterpillars hatch
Eating their shells and milkweed leaves
Watch them grow bigger daily
Spin a silk mat
Hanging upside down
In a green chrysalis
The chrysalis breaks
Out pops a beautiful monarch
With soft, wet wings
Adult flies off
The wings have dried
New adults spend summer
Eat and lay eggs
Winter approaches
Time to migrate
Life cycle repeats itself.

Gail Korndoerfer
Browns Mills, NJ

Don't Cry for Me

Don't cry for me.
I heard your voice as I closed my hazed eyes.
In the darkness, it gave me comfort and courage,
And when I woke, my pain was gone.
A distant light pierced the emptiness,
Illuminating the way to those from our past.
Familiar faces welcomed me home.
Their loving touch wiped away my tears,
And in the midst of love, I remembered you.
Silence broke when He proclaimed,
"Do not cry, for I have given you a gift.
The world of pain has passed and glory awaits you.
One day they will join you again
And hand in hand you will walk through my kingdom.
Until their time, you will watch and protect them."
His gentle touch put me at ease.
My soul has been set free.
I will be with you every day,
Watching and guiding you home
To a place of peace and love
Where we will walk hand in hand through eternity,
So don't cry for me.

Carla C. Allega
Richfield, OH

Praise Him

We go through a lot of things,
And life can be so hard.
You've tried everything else,
Why not try God?
He always has a reason,
And He'll always have a purpose.
Sometimes you don't know why,
But His reason will come to surface.
You probably made plans,
And it's a known fact.
You may think your plans are good,
But God's got something better than that.
Sometimes He'll make you wonder,
Because you're one of the chosen few.
You must have faith,
And patience is a virtue.
Our minds move fast,
And we think so hard.
You can think about a lot of things,
But you can't outthink God.
You're still in the working,
So stand proud and tall.
God doesn't call prepared individuals,
He prepares the individuals He calls.
So keep your trust in God,
Because you're not out on a limb.
He'll supply all your needs,
Just lift your hands and praise Him.

Kevin Caesar
Long Beach, CA

The Pilot

I want Jesus to be my Pilot,
For my life belongs to Him.
When my tiny vessel shudders, driven on the sea of sin.
It's then I cry aloud, "Jesus, save me now."
The disciples frightened to the core
Was a far distance from the shore,
The mighty wind whipped them all about.
Even though it was still afloat,
Reckless waves pounded the little boat.
In troubled plight, Jesus was awakened to their delight.
Knowing they doubted, fought common fears,
Jesus commanded the raging sea with a mighty sound.
The sea obeyed His will when He whispered, "Peace be still."
Turbulent shoals abound on every hand,
On my tiny vessel's deck, I cannot stand.
The waves toss me to and fro,
Alone, I cannot go.
When I try to pilot my own boat,
I flounder, sink, or try to swim.
The Master of the sea must be Master of me.
He alone is in control, no matter what you think.
The raging river is final,
Everyone must cross that shore, some now while others wait.
Let Heaven's own Pilot escort you
As you near the Pearly Gates.

Steve O. Zink
Ardmore, OK

Had I not had parents that took the time to teach reading to a struggling child, I would not have the ability to read and write. My first reading was around the family alter reading the King James version of the Bible. Also, our father gave us drills on Saturday mornings from the McGuffy Readers. My wish is to recognize Rev. Ernest P. & Rev. Norene Zink for their dedication to education.

A Loyal Friend

I feel His presence
I talk to Him in the early
part of the day
When I have done wrong,
I say, "I'm sorry, Lord"
He forgives my sin
He cares about me
when I am sick and even when
there's no total freedom from pain
I whisper His name . . . and He hears
He is my loyal friend
and from deep within
even when there's no total
arrangement between difficulties and ease
In my heart, on my knees
when tears and clouds
and sunshine's laughter
do not agree
I whisper His name
He hears and gives
consideration to my plea.

Helen Roark
Coal City, WV

Untitled

As it is stated
You are known
By the company
You keep

We walk side by side
Take our measured steps
One by one
Same way
Same distance
I look over
To see the face
I see it but I see no features
I hear its voice
And I listen
But I hear no words
I stretch my hand
For its feel of its hand
I reach to no grasp
I look around for the
Company I keep
And suddenly
I know its name
The name of the company I keep
It's loneliness

Betty Bricker
El Paso, TX

How to Be Happy

It's nice to know as each day dawns
God looks down and gives a big yawn
He takes up a vigil and keeps me in mind
My day is busy and to be real kind
My friends are happy to be with me
I think it's my smile they like to see
So if you are blue and not content to be
Just smile a lot and you'll be happy.

Mary Ann Leeper
Leon, IA

Love

A kiss of heaven
For what the Lord has proven
To begin the day again
Whenever your heart awakens
Remembering the joy of birds' song
And as the sun will shine upon

Watching you from wings
Breathing life's kiss
Be loving hearts in tears
Kissing days ahead
Always being true.

Lauren Kurchak
Lakewood, CO

Going Home

Flying back home to Ireland
on the plane with people wearing
Jell-O green trousers and
shamrocked shirts and skirts.
We stop at Shannon and
I get off the plane.
Drop to the tarmac and
kiss the ground.
It's cool and damp like the morning earth.
Get a Guinness
and go on our way.
Fields below us are crazy quilts
of infinite patchwork
peeking through the clouds.
Get off at Dublin
and go through customs.
No problem here, I'm Irish.
How long you staying, they ask.
"Dunno. I'm here to bury m'da."
I go on through,
and the mountains jump up
to wrap their arms around me.
It's the only place that does
to let me know I'm home.

Deirdre Morris
Sun City West, AZ

Happiness

Happiness is a wonderful thing,
you never know when it will spring.
You could be blue,
but where is the clue?
Don't fret long—
before you know it,
it will be gone.
Happiness is always there,
sometimes we just need to clean the air.

Dorene Cook
Davenport, IA

Snowball

I had a dog friend named Snowball
She belonged to my friend Randy
Snowball would lick my face
Snowball and I went every place
One day Snowball looked fat
Randy said Snowball was having puppies
Then I was told Snowball had died
I sat by a bush and cried and cried
The bush started to wiggle
I heard Randy call
And out from the bush came a little Snowball.

Mel Seidl
Middleton, WI

What If?

What if I were a robot
With parts that came apart
With dials and tangled cords
Working to run my heart?

Would I still feel this sadness?
Be tormented by this pain?
If I become a mindless machine
Would life become more sane?

What if a round metal button
Could turn me off and on
And I could take in a program
To make me glad that you have gone?

Would I still feel this emptiness
This reluctance to set you free?
If my heart was cold dull metal
Could you still get through to me?

What if I were a robot
Programmed to act as I do?
Could someone pull a wire
And then I'd forget you?

Or would I break into pieces
Totally fall apart?
Lie in pieces on the floor
A robot with a broken heart.

Barbara Davey
Chicago, IL

Death's Angel

You will never know when
Will I come in the dark of night,
Or maybe in the early morn,
When the dew is still in flight.

Maybe while you sleep, with
The hush of a warm breeze
Coming through your window,
Making the curtains blow free.

You will never know
When I come, or from
Where I come.

Iola Burns
Williamstown, NJ

I studied music in Main, Germany. I taught for thirty-five years and always wanted to write. I love to write little poems and read. My lighthouses are my hobby.

Sin

Is it a sin, the glide of your hand as it traces my breast?
The harmony of your fingers as they dance
The contours of my body?
The hitch in my breathing when it all starts?
The whisper of flesh against flesh?
My learning, my delight in the exploration
Of your body?
The promise of pleasure that I can give you?
These things bespeak of our passion, our hunger.
Are they sinful?
Your soft touch whispered endearments, those millions of
Small things,
You, all mirrors of similarity.
Those things whisper of our love.
That point that each of us at some point reaches . . .
When it's only you and I, and nothing keeps our flesh apart.
Fulfillment.
If it's a sin I am choosing to live, then live it I will,
For surely loving without a little sin is only a
Faded reproduction of what God had in
Mind.

Rachel Feltaous
Truth or Consequences, NM

Freedom

Freedom.
It is fought for by slaves,
It is used by those that live in caves.
In the sitting city
Is where the pity
Arises and stays,
For those without it,
They fall into a great pit
And become slaves themselves.

Freedom,
For those some
When it comes around,
They will leave their berth.
They will rise above the Earth.
They will join the clouds,
And they will look down on the crowds.
They will call down,
And invite the others to the hoedown
That comes with freedom.

Joseph Conrad
Fairfield, CA

Airport Coffee

Those steady mountains made me think
just a little too much as the plane
touched down five minutes early due
to a tailwind and some kind of
curvy magic. I want to ask, did you
know my favorite color is green today
but will be blue tomorrow?
Or something simpler,
like Did Albert Einstein ever go by Al?
But instead we sit,
wait, my fingers twitching on
the armrest as I watch the sunlight
splintering off the left wing, glittering
pieces that make my eyes, both tired
and contemplative, old and young.

Melisha Garrett
Cleveland, TN

Life of Liberty

America, we stand so proud and free.
We, the people, stand our ground for a life of liberty.
Our child pays for the sins of you and me.
Let's raise our heads, see their need to live a life of liberty.

God must bow His head to look across this land
To see the child at the mercy of sin's great hand,
Abusing and killing the ones that need us most.
Let's look and see their need, no matter what the cost.

Miss Liberty stands so tall and free,
She holds her head high with a life of liberty.
If we look close, we'll see a tear—she cries for you and me.
Her heart breaks for her child caught in all the adversity.

America, help your child stand up proud and free
So they can live a life of liberty.
God will raise His head to look at you and me
To see His child have the life that was meant to be.

America, help your child have a life of liberty.

Doris Whisnant
Morganton, NC

A Talk Needed

I wish you could come down from Heaven
And talk to me once more.
There's so many things I'd say to you
That I should have said before.
I'd say I loved you
Every day of the year,
And all the things about you
That I hold so very dear.
I'd say you worked too hard
And deserve a rest.
I'd take you places
That you loved the best.
I'd tell you I'm so lonely
Since you've been gone,
And how I miss your love.
I no longer welcome the dawn.
I'd tell you my love is still true
And there's no one in my world but you.
I'd say my life revolved around you
For you made my every wish come true.
I thank God for giving us the time
When I was yours
And you were mine.

Doran Meadows
Clarkdale, AZ

You Would Be There

I was born and
You would be there
Then I became older, got in trouble and
You would be there
I did things fun and some crazy and
You would be there
I grew and grew and
You would be there
I finally got married and
You would be there
I grew up
And you would be there
Every day something new happened and
You would be there
Then that day was bad because God needed you instead and
You were not here
You would be there
In my life things change
You will still be there
You are a part of me always and
You will always and forever be there!

Michelle Gentile
St. Joseph, MO

A Day to Remember

A year ago today,
you took our precious loved
ones away.
You were cruel and heartless
in everything you did.
You tried so very hard
to tear out nation apart,
but the one thing you did
was to bring our people closer
in heart.
For a while, our lives, you
tore apart,
but you helped us get a
little bit smart.
God is in our lives, never
to part.
You think you've won the
battle, but that is not so,
for with the help of God,
the light is green to go.
So when you did this
cruel thing, God sent His heavenly dove
to take your precious loved ones
to be with Him above.
So in all that you have done,
our nation and our people
have become one.

Theresa A. Dement
Jacksonville, NC

Old Shabby House

Old shabby house
Almost beyond repair,
What are you thinking
As you're standing there?
Are you longing for the good days
That have passed you by,
Days when you stood up proud
Silhouetting the morning sky?
Now, just look at you . . . half-standing,
Thinking of the past.
You're a deserted, crumbling, molding
State of contrast.
You have a rotting, leaking roof,
And warping, creaking floors.
You have broken, shattered windows,
And falling, leaning doors.
Why were you left standing like this
In such a sad, forgotten state?
Are your owners coming to repair you?
Why did they wait so late?
Could it be they've passed to a better house,
Somewhere beyond the blue?
If they're never returning, my old friend,
What will happen to you?

Rose Dyess Anderson
Ellisville, MS

I was born in Laurel, Mississippi. I graduated from Ellisville High School and attended William Carey College, the University of Southern Mississippi, and Alcorn State University. I taught school in Natchez, Mississippi for thirty-seven years. I am married to Talmadge Anderson. We have one son and four grandsons. I traveled from Natchez to Ellisville to visit my parents for a number of years. I traveled through the little town of Silver Creek. There, beside the road, stood a stately old decaying house that spurred my curiosity, so I was motivated by it to write the poem, "Old Shabby House."

Obama's Katrina

The Gulf oil disaster
seeping angry death
towards the beautiful
beaches and habitats
along our southern
shores.

Karen A. Pierson
Galeburg, IL

Emotional Pain

Without you I'm going insane
The emotional pain is setting into my brain
When I wake up I just wish the pain would drain
You're like the pain reliever
And I am your believer
I wanna be closer
And I wanna be the boaster
When I am around you
My love is strong
But when away
I just wanna be gone
This is my emotional pain

Tannor Fortin
Derby, VT

The Hope Is Close

My friend,
There is no end.
Glimpse the reason
This is sent.
Try then.
Where going, tense
Believing this is meant.
The hope is close,
Like someone's ghost
That loves you most.
On this rough road,
You'll gain your soul
From those who stole.
In vain, you don't,
In vain, you don't.

Nathaniel C. Preiss
Sarasota, FL

Nighttime

Daylight is slowing ebbing. The dark fingers of night are pushing, pulling, sweeping the last flickers of light over the western horizon. Daylight has not given up the fight easily, extending its last brilliant rays toward the darkness and then bursting into an unparalleled mass of color, as though making a bold statement that it would not be gone forever.

The darkness of the night has totally enveloped the landscape, as though a dark cape was flung over the Earth, still warm from the departed sunlight. An encompassing change of mood ensues. The fear of the darkness paralyzes a few. The freedom of being released from a day of toil delights others. The evil forces are released, sleeking through the shadows to achieve sometimes unspeakable evils upon the unweary. The limitless expanse of the heavens is slowly illuminated with an endless array of stars, like millions of sparkling diamonds. The moon emerges full and bright, adding a dim light to the utter darkness. The presence of these heavenly bodies seems to ignite a flurry of romance. Hands caress. Lips part and tenderly melt together, promoting a blending of love, passion, and excitement.

With a minimal amount of resistance, the darkness is slowly pushed aside. A new day emerges, splashing pale shades of pink and blue across the sky. The sun bumps the moon aside, replacing it in the heavens with a burning brilliance. The endless cycle is again repeating itself. Nighttime has elicited many changes and challenges to be faced as this new day emerges.

Did you hear the daybreak or see the nightfall?

Rosemary Reno
Powell, WY

To You

Who is he? What is he
That my soul commends him?
Handsome, sweet, and courteous is he,
A rose so red did bloom upon him
That shines gravely beneath
Is he kind as he seems?
For the love I leave between
In my eyes he sees
To make him see the love that gleams
In my heart that be
To him my heart sings
That he is charming
He expands each precious thing
In my heart that burns
To him my love will yearn.

Akila Rabsatt
Jacksonville, FL

A Friend

You're a friend so kind and dear,
Always close, far or near
Just thinking about you,
What a special person you are,
And how the world is because
You are a good friend
You are a person I know
Has changed my life in some way
Through a simple conversation,
A warm hug, or making a statement
Having you in my life
Has helped me grow and heal
Laugh, love, learn, and smile
The blessings never end
As God has allowed our paths to cross
With families and friends,
So please know that this poem
Is more than a wish
Thank you for being on my list
Enjoy your time in everything you do
Remember, God loves you and I do too.

Margaret Ray
Stanford, KY

The Cowman

A cowman's day begins at dawn,
It matters not the weather.
His world is full of things to do
To make his cow herd better.
But feeding is his favorite chore,
He'd never want to quit it.
He knows they love him every day
'Cause they run to him to get it.

Sara Jo Renfroe
Toppenish, WA

Untitled

Inspired by a real couple, good friends of a good friend of mine

Art and Pam aren't drinking beer
Not to celebrate their fortieth year.
Champagne is what they're going to drink
So fill their glasses to the brink.
Years that brought them joy and woe
But always with a place to go.
The comfort of each other's arms
Where not a soul could do them harm.
So raise your glass and make a toast
Forty years is something to boast!

Peggy Slowinski
Amherst, NY

Childhood Days

Oh, to relive childhood
Wishes
Of simple dreams and mud
Pie dishes.
To let one's mind take
You away
With grand castles to
Play all day.

Magda Rothkehl
Vacaville, CA

Push

Sometimes it becomes too much weight
Time, it's not worth the wait
Burdens heavy, but you can see the light
Just dig deep, push with all your might
Progress, at times, can become slow
Almost to a stop, and you want to lose hope
Burdens still heavy, but you don't want to stop
You just have to push, you can see the top
Just bow your head, let your heart pray
Not just when in need, but every day
Enlighten your soul and shed the weight
Push toward Him and trust your faith.

Andre Simpson
Knoxville, TN

A College of Angels

There must be a college in Heaven where angels learn to fly
And someday I'll be called upon to climb those steps up high
When the angels come for me and take me home,
Those golden gates I'll see
In the distance not far beyond, a college waits for me
Inside the gates, angels greet me one by one,
Their wings of gold so huge and bright
My eyes can't believe such a glorious sight
Waiting to be picked and then to learn in the college of angels best
There I will get my wings and learn to fly,
For then I will be like all the rest
I'll stand so proud among the clouds and spread my golden wings
I'll sing so loud while waiting to be called
To do God's earthly things
Not all the angels will have wings, you see
For in God's master plan, some must stay behind,
For what must be will be
When I'm called on to take that journey home,
You'll know when I'm around
For I will wrap my wings around you,
Pick you up when you're feeling down
Then when God decides to call you home, you will surely know I'm near
For I will be the one to guide you there
All the angels will come to greet you with outstretched golden wings
And a glorious song for you we'll sing
For now you are in God's place of love and eternal rest
Like me, you'll have earned your wings in the college of angels best.

Anne H. Rousseau
Eustis, ME

Diamond Dust

Walk outside this early morning and dumbstruck by what lay before my eyes.
Diamond dust!
Diamond dust lay glittering and sparkling clear across the yard.
Oh, the riches I have! I walk in marvel among the glinting diamonds.
Perhaps my eyes were deceived by the sparkle,
but not a single prism was to be seen,
not a single shade of rainbow.
Just a vast sea of diamond dust.
Wait, there by the tree. Do you not see?
Emeralds! Ahh, more riches!
Emeralds lay scattered around the trunk. A clump of frozen grass, you say!
Psshh, emeralds I say.
Emeralds laid softly against the wonder of wonders!
The great gold bark of the tree. No ostentatious glint and glitter of
jewels here,
no, but the soft deep glow for this wondrous fellow.
Gold reaching from the ground to the beautiful sapphire sky.
Ahhh, do you not now wish for the riches I have?

Patricia Shelton
Kingman, AZ

Look at Me

Look at me!
I'm a shining star.
I'm involved in a lot of things,
Don't you think I'll go far?
I'm the cream of the crop,
One of the best.
In everything I do,
I beat all the rest.
When I'm older, I'll be famous,
Everyone will know my name.
When it comes to describing me,
No one uses the word "lame."
But even with all my riches
And all of my fame,
It will all be nothing
If I don't remember Christ's name.
You know, it's funny
How people are.
One day they're the devil
And suddenly they're a star.
They should be ashamed,
Claiming all the fame,
Playing their evil games,
Making sure everyone knows their name.
I think they just want attention,
You know how people are.
One day they're the devil,
And suddenly they're a star.

Kayla Snow
Okolona, MS

Asunder

Though in my dream I wonder
On how my love may grow,
For this magic thunders
Amidst a love so cold.
For if a man be stronger,
And wants to mend a soul,
Should he gather much asunder
Forever now to hold?
I cannot tell you, brother,
Of all the things I've done,
But just imagine, angel,
Thy work beneath my thumb.
Can notes foretell your future?
Can Man predict his death?
Among the leaves He travels,
But He considers not his breath,
Or would He touch another,
Only to be betrayed
Among his brothers daily
Who never knew his way?
I ask you now, my friend,
What wisdom flows within,
And even deep bloods weary
There is no real weeping sin.

Wendy Samples
Hanceville, AL

Love

The farther away I get,
the closer I get to you.
With each fleeing day, I want
to capture it and savor it
forever.
The rapture of my heart
speaks words of magic I've
never known.
Speak softly, my love, for
words mirror in my soul
to say, "Be still, and listen to
your very heart, for it speaks.
In the rush of things, sometimes
we don't take time to ponder
and think." I sit very quiet, and
it speaks to me saying,
"Your heart has touched mine,
and mine yours."
To laugh, to feel, to touch
and to love . . . I found in you.

Marian Sloan
Trafford, PA

Thank You, Lord

Thank You, Lord, for the smile upon my face.
Thank You, Lord, for Your love and amazing grace.
Thank You, Lord, for all You've done for me.
Thank You, Lord, for Calvary.
Thank You, Lord, for a new heart.
Thank You, Lord, for a new start.
Thank You, Lord, for loving me.
Thank You, Lord, for letting me see.
Thank You, Lord, for calling me home.
Thank You, Lord, for I'll never have to roam.
Thank You, Lord, for showing me love.
Thank You, Lord, for Heaven above.
Thank You, Lord, for being with me.
Thank You, Lord, for my family.
Thank You, Lord, for all You do.
Thank You, Lord, for guiding me through.
Thank You, Lord, for Your healing touch,
For I have never been loved so much.

Shelby J. Simpson
Burlington, NC

Untitled

Should I apologize
I've waited for the chance
Should I forgive
Is this our last dance
Should I look away
Should I remember all that you had to say
Can I just get over it
Will these feelings ever go away
I am lost to his voice
My body's in his hands
I am filled up with love
I didn't stand a chance
It's everything about him that I love most of all
Like when he lays me down
And protects me from the fall
I know what I am
It's not hard to see
I am infatuated
I swear he's all I need.

Michelle M. Sutton
Maysville, NC

The Weaver

The weaver sat down to weave one day
A garment of beauty rare.
Each thread did yield completely
To His touch of loving care.
Back and forth the shuttle did fly,
The pattern began to show.
It was a thing of beauty
As He wove it row upon row.
The threads began to show signs of strain
And rebelled at the Master's touch,
Then knotted and tangled they became,
This pattern was just too much!
Then with strong but gentle hands
The weaver took the strings.
He pulled them here and there a bit
And they yielded once again.
And so sometimes our lives become
So filled with little things.
The Master weaver must stop His work
And untangle the knotted strings.
And though it seems so hard to yield
To a pattern we can't see,
Yet the Master weaver, He does know
What the finished work will be.

Mary S. Schwamb
Selma, CA

Death at My Door

Knock, knock.
Who's there! No one answers
so I walk to the door. I looked through
The peephole only to see darkness on
this bright and sunny day.
Knock! Knock! Knock!
Who are you?
I'm Death at your door!
Go away! Go away! I need his soul.
Let him go! Let him go!
He doesn't need to suffer anymore.
I hate you! I hate you, Death at my door!
You will not have his soul.
Knock! Knock! Knock!
(Let him go!)
My heart aches to say these words.
I will let him go only if you come in the dark
of the night, and not on this bright
sunny day to take his soul.
I hate you, Death at my door,
and yes, he doesn't need to suffer
anymore.

Mary Ruth Spinola
Rio Rancho, NM

"Death at My Door" was so real I wouldn't let him come in. I know he was there! My husband was dying—no turning it back, but I took care of him all my life as a wife of forty-two years. When we met in the third grade, we fell in love at first sight. I had to let him go. He suffered so much until he saw that I won't let go. Until death knocked at my door, I knew it was time to let go. My husband saw my eyes and soon let go and went with death at our door.

Peace to All

May creed nor color bring neither a door or a shudder.
Can pride of the insecure bring peace that is pure?
Could some believe and some not be sure?
Only time will tell as we have cast our lure.
These things we pray only God can endure.
May this be put to pass with a feeling that is secure.

Ronald E. Smith
Longview, TX

The Learning Hike

Learning is like a mountain awaiting someone to climb it.
When you learn, you are hiking in your mind's mountain.
Learning is like an old hiker's path just waiting for new hikers
to climb up it.
Learning for most is a constant uphill battle.
When you learn, you deepen the trail of knowledge you have.
The first and last step are going to be the most challenging.
All the middle is going to depend on the effort you put in it.
The effort you put in is the triumph of failure you receive.
The final product of hiking and learning should and will
look very different.
In the end, learning is like a very wonderful hike!

Gunnar Merkel
Liberty Lake, WA

Unbearable

Stranded, useless, wasting
away, dreaming of a more
fulfilling day.
Love has come and now it's
gone.
Heart is melting, burning,
never to beat again.
Thump, thump, thump, I have
flatlined, like the freshest corpse
with its skin still soft.
Gasping, gasping for air,
hand clutched upon my chest.
As I lie upon a bed, close
my eyes, and there you be
like an angel looking down at me.
Days will turn to months,
to years, and I scream with
every breath; because of
you, my life is unbearable.

Jennifer Todeschini
Catasauqua, PA

Embers of Love

Oh, but the hands of time,
Through silver locks they wind.
Bonnie, Bonnie, your eyes of blue,
Bygone have never weathered their hue.
Somewhat stooped, still reaching out,
Your soul has experienced what life's about.
The embers of love still all aglow,
The hearts of some may never know.

Karen Templeton
Montrose, PA

A Candle

The lady ignited on her cage,
A spark of light gave her presence on stage.
She began to dance, she looked so free,
But his is not a sanctuary.
She sways right as the wind blows her frame,
And as it halts, she feels herself tame.
The cream stage progresses further down,
Melting and pulling her scarlet gown.
Dripping and slipping won't stop this dance,
Beauty knows it's the very last chance.
Almost as suddenly as it began,
Smoke says goodbye to our greatest fan.

Lindsey Griswold
Williamsburg, VA

Untitled

I sit in my room, black as the abyss.
Every day I sense something is amiss.
Do I wonder or just not care? For me to know is oddly rare.
These feelings that I feel are just so unreal.
Deep inside I feel the stress, for it doesn't go away with rest.
My dreams are haunted, I'm silenced and bound.
I don't hear a single sound.
I look around, but all I see is black.
Patience is the one thing I lack.
I struggle to get free, just to hear "Your freedom shall never be."
Nobody's there that I can see.
With one final assault, I break the chains.
I sit up and fight through the pains.
I close my eyes and as they open, I return to my life that is so broken.
I have beaten my demons for now.
They will soon return, for this war is not over.

Adam Thomas
Kissimmee, FL

The Military Escort

By the graveside we silently wait
in the wind and the cold of the day.
An old soldier is called to his fate
and to him our respects we will pay.
Down the road the lights on the hearse
bring a shuffle of feet in the snow.
It signals the time to disperse
to our assignment that each of us know.
The flag-covered casket is borne
to the vault lying deep in the ground.
Friends and family huddle forlorn,
only breeze-carried flakes make a sound.
In crisp air the shots loudly snap
while little ones cover their ears.
The tone of mournful blown "Taps"
with its low distant echo brings tears.
The flag from the casket is lifted
and made into a triangular fold.
I walk where the path is less drifted
to the loved one our regrets there are told.
"On behalf of a grateful nation," I say,
and the look in her eyes makes me pause.
"We present you the flag this day,
under which our comrade served a great cause."

Robert W. Teeples
Black River Falls, WI

Sunny Day Fun

Outside it is a sunny day
for fun and to play
The sun is high up in the Sky
to stay for the day
Cold drinks ready on a tray
on a warm sunny day
To be here and to say
"What a nice sunny day"
Fun in the sun
and to play
Out in the backyard
for today
Near the lake and
the dock and bay
Throwing a beach ball
up and to each other
and out and away
The radio and music are
heard and singing far away
Sport boats speeding through
the water and the bays
on the sunny fun day!

Diana Thorpe
Rochester, MN

Key to My Heart

Look up, look down, look all around
Where will the key to my heart be found?
Will it be in my garden of flowers so bright
Kissed by the dew of the morning light?
Or perhaps under the sky of blue,
In a field of clover that we walked through?
Could it be in the swing where we held hands,
And talked of the future and made promises and plans!
Have you looked in my eyes so brown,
And seen them shine whenever you're around!
If you have done all this, then you already know
You found the key to my heart, for I love you so.
And as years pass by and we walk by side,
We will smile and say with pride
Our life has been wonderful right from the start.
Thank you for finding the key to my heart.

Peggy Traeger
Estill Springs, TN

I Wish to Fly

I wish to be a butterfly
With multicolor wings
To fly deep, deep in the sky
Where nobody can see.
I'll take with me in the blue sky
The war, the sickness, and the pain.
I'll fly with that so far, so deep
And bring the hope again.
We fight, we hate, we run away
We all forget to love.
This little word is so immense
Can change so fast the world.
Nobody cares that we want peace,
We want to love, we want to play.
Where is the hope of growing old
With magic times and liberty?
I wish to be a butterfly
To bring the joy of life,
Flying up, deep in the blue sky,
Sending light and love on my way up.
We need the light, we need the love,
It's all we want, it's all we need.
The time is running out so fast,
We all forgot to blink.
We need to pause and taste the life,
Look in the sky to see the butterfly.

Gabi Touchette
Earleville, MD

Reflections of a Mom and Nurse

As I've entered my golden years of life
I reflect back to my years as a nurse and wife
A mom of six of whom we lost one
a son from an accident whose
life was too soon done
As I started my life as a
nurse in spite of my fears
due to the health of my
husband of twenty years
I think of all that has happened to me
and to all my kids, grandkids, and family
but as a nurse, I hope I have helped someone
before my life on Earth is done
I have loved my life as mom and nurse
the time I've spent helping
those who are worse
We are all nurses in life, it seems
taking care of our family and all our dreams
We face fears every day that
we are doing right
by our family and friends with all our might
but as I come to the end
of my life with these reflections and dreams
I continue to work at all of these things
May God help me be to the end of my days
the best kind of mom
and nurse always.

Betty L. Orender
Topeka, KS

The Roof

Trudging through a
green pasture
wondering what will
happen after death.
My life has been
hidden under a roof
of grief and sadness.
I feel like I'm
hidden inside a
dark, treacherous cave.
A fog awaits my
presence. Will
I pass through the
fog without any issues,
or will the fog
take a toll in my life?

Kristin Webb
Sebring, FL

Mother Nature

She is born
Blossoming like a flower in nature's womb
Her body floats like that of a butterfly
Serene deep in beauty
Her eyes are of the world
Taking in everything good and bad
Her debonair manner ripe and fresh
She moves throughout the universe
Like a mother of young
All the way caring and protecting
Her smile is one of the sun
Bright and warm
Covering the Earth while heating the cold
Her heart is the protector
Fighting survival
It's the way of nature herself
She's natural
Like summer rain and sunshine
Yet embraced within ice and cold
She endureth Man

Lori Wallace
Aurora, MO

My Memories of Snead State College

As the summer days are coming to the end
and now its scent a memory of the lazy days of summer,
a touch of fall fills the cool, crisp
breeze coming across Snead State College campus.
For many students just starting for the first time,
it's going to be a challenge for both young students
and older students as well.
It's going to take me a little longer
to learn my way around the campus and keep my classes straight.
It's time for everybody to settle down
and start studying for their choice of courses,
such as computer two thousand and seven classes, Word,
also Power Point and other classes.
These two years, I have been studying for my degree.
It is quickly coming to a close.
We all have become a family and very supportive
staff members, how loving, caring;
also compassionate upon students who have special needs.
They help students in all areas of their work.
I finished Snead College with honors, and at age sixty,
it will always be cherished as personal goal
and dream come true for me.

Sherry A. Warren
Albertville, AL

The Kiss

Every time I see a couple kissing,
It's you and me that I see.
I see and want and feel and want, and
remember and want that sweet kiss,
that sweet kiss you always gave to me.

Oh, dear God, how I want to feel that
sweet kiss again
to show my love for him, and he shows
his love for me.
I miss him so much, his tenderness,
that magic in our kiss.
I thank You, Lord, for bringing him to
me, for making him mine.
Our life together started with a kiss,
sealed with a kiss, and ended with a kiss,
the kiss that I sorely miss.

Martha E. Wilson
Sierra Vista, AZ

Windows from My Soul

I dare peep through?
For I'm older now, a little
higher up my tree. I look,
I see beautiful hands
splashed with the touch
of flour, ready and so
steady for the crust of
life to be laid down so gently.
I watch in awe
as the berries are
poured, spilling into the
crust of life that has
just been made.
So sweet, the taste,
the smell, as if a new day
just arrived,
for I am there!
If only in my tree of
life
I see through the
windows of my soul,
and I remember!

Judy Welch
Dexter, ME

I was born on March 9, 1956 and am the youngest of seven—five brothers, one sister. I grew up in Garland, Maine, a small town on Oliver Hill. My father was a truck driver and my mother was a stay-at-home mom who also wrote. I was a single mom at eighteen with one son and was married once at thirty-three. Since 1987, I have been a certified nursing assistant in nursing homes. My childhood memories inspired me, the good and not so good—a form of healing, I think. I wrote a letter to my mom after she passed. It all came out in poetry form, though I didn't realize it until I read all eight pages of it. I am forever grateful for you reading and choosing my poem. I am living my dream of being a poet.

Wrestling Meet

The whistle blows and my heart starts pounding.
The muscles tense and the blood starts to flow.
It's the roar of the crowd that I hear sounding
Off the walls that makes the muscles grow.

Two competitors standing face to face and toe to toe.
Heart and desire could be the factors that
Allow me the chance to slip the collar and elbow,
Shoot that single leg and put my opponent on the mat.

For the next several minutes, we roll round and round,
Each wrestler trying to gain the advantage.
Take down, reversal, near fall points found,
Each point earned gets me closer to center stage.

The thrill of victory, or the agony of defeat
Will be discovered at every wrestling meet.

Dillon White
Glen Burnie, MD

Gardening

Oh, the heat wave
Throw down the hoe
Let the weeds grow

Unbutton the blouse
Blow down the neckline
Make the air stir

Tie back the hair
Sleeve-pat the brow
Fan the skirt

Head for the trees
Plop in the hammock
Whistle for the wind

Stretch the legs
Spread the arms
Hope for a breeze

Drink lemonade
Finger dip the ice
Drip drops

Margaret Whitman
Jacksonville, NC

Haven

There's a haven within my soul, lifting me higher as I greet
the Lord each day. I share with Him my every thought, word, and
deed. He knows my every sin and sorrow, yet His love always constant.
Without You, Lord, I am nothing. With You, Lord, I am something.
When all seems lost, I go to the haven within my soul, a restoration
of peace, love, and tranquility.
Come, Holy Spirit, enshroud me into the fire of my Lord, a facade of
protection.
There's a haven within my soul, lifting me higher as I greet the Lord
each day. I cry for help as I struggle to survive life's ups and downs.
Understanding these burdens is a confusing and sometimes lonely
search, but with the Lord's love, I know I will survive.
Retreating to the haven within my soul, I find a restoration of peace,
love, and tranquility.
There's a haven within my soul, lifting me higher as I greet
the Lord each day. Lord, am I needed by those around me, or am
I just tolerated? Barriers are everywhere. How do I overcome?
Lord, as I reach out to You, protect me in the fire of Your love.
Without You, Lord, I am nothing. With You Lord, I am something.
You are the haven within my soul!

Marta L. Warnke
Carroll, IA

Upon the Passing of One So Dear

We resign ourselves to it as an unavoidable fact to face,
Yet we still feel quite down when one so dear
departs this earthly place.
We know that one gets older and declines after a rise,
yet with one we love so dear, we feel something about life to despise.

As facets of life seem to recycle over and over again,
we seriously wonder, through reincarnation, if one lives again,
for upon the passing of one so dear in our admiration,
how nice it would be to have that one again through reincarnation.

Be they male or female, we have all cherished a person so dear,
yet we still feel insure on the thought of a passing of one so dear.
Regardless of the disheartening cold
and the dark, eerie gloom of the night,
the one we liked so dear provided
the friendship, the warmth, and the light.

It's been said that if we have fond memories of people so dear
that for as long as we live of these people so dear,
we, in a sense, keep ourselves young in spite of an occasional tear
with fond memories of people so dear that seem crystal clear.

Alan R. Leake
Bennington, VT

May

Drunk on the wild plum,
heady with endless stretches
of bluebells surrendered to the woods
(such are spring's goods,
not to sell, but to sate
novice eyes so long accustomed to the late
gray winter's moods);

all, all is given from these places
where you oh, Trinity, hide your faces.

Eileen Haugh
Rochester, MN

Search

Mysteries are often deep
and undisturbed,
and then one day someone
pulls back the curtains of
their imagination and dares to
peep at the unknown.
How surprise they must be to
discover that I am there.
Creator and sustainer,
the I Am that I Am.

Joyce Williams
Anthony, FL

Dear Mom

May we always cherish each day that we can be with you
It's the ties that bind and your countless gift of love
For it's your love that keeps us going
Yes, you smiled at me when I was born
It's the love between a mother and her child
And all those countless gifts of love
You were always there for us, no matter what
For you have sheltered us in the storms of life
And from our mother's arms, you have blessed us on our way
Your countless gifts of love are still with us today
It's a blessing we have you for our mom
For we should count our many blessings
And tell you that we love you, Mom
For it was your hands that rocked the cradle when we were born
It's the joy we share that none other has known
I can see it more clearly now, Mom
Yes, morning has broken of a brand-new day
For you have left footprints in the sand and in my heart
And they are there for me to follow you
For you have blessed me on my way
What more can I asked for, a mother's love
For you have given me life
We should thank God for creating mothers
For you are very precious and dear to all of us
Mom, we love you from the bottom of our hearts

Louise Heimlich
Delaware, OH

My Love

Every time I look into your eyes
It makes me pray for no goodbyes
You to me are the only one
When we are together
There is nothing but fun
No matter what the weather
Or what the day brings
I wish to you
The most wonderful things
If there comes a day
When we must part
Deep down inside
You will be in my heart
But for now
I can truly say
I love you
In every way!

Aaron J. Hart
Dawson Springs, KY

Your Ivory Towers

When you look into the eyes of the one
do you see a sparkle like the sun golden rays?
As you hold your love very tight soon you will
know that it is your love you want to praise.
Yes, you will know that it is the love just for
you as in your heart you will hear this phrase.
Yes, my dear, you are the love of my life,
yes, the one I want with me all the rest of my days.
Don't let the darkness of a cloudy night hide
the stars that into your life will brightly shine,
that will light the eyes of the one that you
want to ask, will you always be truly mine?
Yes, look past the shadows of darkness that you
wonder why it seems to be there all the time.
Oh, my, look at the smile of your love that is
like the loving words of a poem that is sublime.
Don't think of the endless nights and days
that seem to have so many lonely hours.
Yes, always think of the times we walked in
the garden and were blessed by the flowers.
Oh, my, look beyond the cold of the snow and
the rain that will bring the endless showers.
Then you will see into the heart of the one
you want to be with in your ivory towers.

David J. Hampson
Greeley, CO

Gift of Love

Our daughter has blessed us
With a baby boy.
He is our grandson and such a joy!
His eyes are green, his hair is blond,
He is a gift from God above.

His smiles have captured
Our hearts and souls.
His tears have left us uncontrolled.
How we lived before his entrance
Has left us pondering
Our mere existence.
Thank You, Lord, our God above,
For gracing us
With our gift of love.

Millie Hirt
Midland, TX

Ole Man and His Dog

As the old man works in his garden each day,
His big red dog tugs on his pant leg wanting to play.
The old man plants his garden each year,
While the job of the dog is to keep out the deer.
The old man plants each seed with care,
Knowing his dog will always be there.
As the old man waters each plant with care,
His red dog smells the odor a passing black bear.
The smell of the garden blows in the wind,
Letting all know that the plants are in.
As the sun shines down on the garden so bright,
The plants will grown into the night.
The old man sits on a rock with his dog by his side,
They watch the garden grow with pride.
At the end of the garden lays an old rotten log,
Behind it digging is a huge groundhog.
The dog spots the critter and runs with grace
To frighten the groundhog out of his place.
The old man grins as he watches his dog
Run though the garden to chase the groundhog.
The plants are growing so tall toward the sun,
While the old man and his dog have had some fun.
The old man and his dog are done for the day,
Both of them will be back tomorrow to work and play.
Night has fallen and it's time to rest;
As the old man looks at his dog, he knows he's the best!

Raymond C. Hoffman
Tamaqua, PA

Alaskan Memories

Plans and trips that are made
With a friend
Make books full of memories
That will never end

Seals and otters, eagles and moose
Jet boat ride and panning for gold
Buses and planes and riding the rail
And Mt. McKinley, so majestic and bold

Rocks and glaciers, oh, what a view
Sunsets on mountains called Alpenglow
Fall colors ablaze in Denali Park
The next morning, we find termination snow

Then it's back on the plane and home we come
With books full of memories that
Will never end
Of a wonderful trip that was shared
With a friend

Carol Hennis
Van Wert, OH

Passage

She lay there soft and still
Beautiful flowers surrounding her everywhere
Everything now is deep down and dead
Taken up to Heaven, by the hand she was led

Marie Hendershot
Black Creek, NC

Rain

This arid land, my home
what beauty.
The moon tonight obscured
by clouds, dark clouds filled with
rain.
Yes, a gentle kiss of rain.
Then torrents fill the gullies. Rain.
I stand in prayer, great
mystery. Merciful healer. Granter
of miracles. Giver of life.
I am but a grain of sand. I turn
my face to You. Your blessing.
Rain.

Naida Orr
Nespelem, WA

Mighty Ohio

Mighty Ohio on the edge of town
How many barges have you seen go down
I'd love to sit upon your sandy shore
In the cool breeze under the stars once more
How many bridges span your mighty tide
To reach from Indiana to the other side
If there any who feel as I
Who love to see the waters roll by
Maybe when we reach our heavenly shore
We'll see the beautiful Ohio River once more

Sharon DeBoard
Hanover, IN

Me!

Some days I wonder who I am,
if I am me or someone else.
I think about the one I am
and in my mind, I'm not myself.
I wonder how all this can be,
then I take a look at me.
I change my mind a dozen times,
then realize that I am me,
the someone else I dare to be.
Me!

Sondra Laporte
Hopkinsville, KY

Come Take My Hand

I stretched out my hand to you
And left it right there,
Waiting for you in your own way
To bring me your cares.

I'm on your side.
I've been there from the start,
For you are my child,
And I love you with all my heart.

I have a plan for you,
But I must take you there.
When you misstep or take a detour,
I'm standing right here.

All you have to do is turn around.
Come back where you're safe.
Just bask in the unending glow
Of my mercy and grace.

For I am your God.
I created you.
Come take my hand,
And I'll see you through.

Evelyn Dove Coleman
Kinston, NC

The Killing Machine

New driver, a teen.
Behind the wheel, she sits like a queen.
In her hand, a talking machine.
Foot on the gas, hand to her ear.
Car automatic, speeding in gear.
Mind far away, perhaps on a date.
Step down harder, don't want to be late.
Beautiful girl, free as a bird.
Slow down, I scream, but I can't be heard.
Far up the road, over a hill,
I hear a crash, my heart stands still.
Traffic is stopping, lights flash ahead.
I remembered her smile as past me she sped.
Heads turn to stare as we slowly crawl by.
I know tonight, a mother will cry.

Rochelle King
San Diego, CA

The Sixth of May

It rained all day yesterday and the new leaves on the trees
Grew as we watched
The creeks and streams and hillside paths stirred and eddied as
The waters flowed downhill

The tree trunks were black against the green
And rain drips fluttered leaves
It's wet this day in May on our home in Tennessee

But today I see that we had missed another lovely sight
Today the dew is heavy on the ground spiders' webs
They appear throughout the forest floor like fairy tents
Left from a great gathering that we were too late to see

Rain drips linger on blades of grass
Like gems or party favors left behind

A fanciful notion to be sure
But one that I believe
For this is what I saw my first May in Tennessee

Dayle Jacob
Monterey, TN

The Long Goodbye

The tests look bad, they told us that day
It's cancer and have to operate
Once that was done, and after chemo
They told us they would do a stem-cell transplant
Hospitalizations, broken bones, and viruses
He is strong, however, and fights for his life
He lives longer than they predict and
Fights with everything that is in him
Then we are given the news that it is back
Back with a vengeance
He is in pain and I am helpless
The medications thankfully dull his pain
We call hospice, a hard decision
Two nice women come for the interview
He makes them smile and their job easier
He tells them that he knows, and is ready
More meds, more surgery
He sleeps a lot and is weak
"I'll just put on my pajamas" he says
And that is not like him
He forgets what day it is and groans as he sleeps
We have a nightly ritual dance of ups and downs
There is no position for him without pain
God help us!
His eyes now closed for two days, he no longer speaks
I love you, I say, go from my arms to God's and suffer no more.

Priscilla Owenby
Marion, NC

Definition

You came taking my love my heart
You left my world falling apart
Striving for the very best
My weary soul at last finds rest
The definition of forgiveness

My life rewinding in the middle of a song
Forgiving what you did me wrong
Holding on to all my grace
Finishing this long hard race
The definition of faith

Forgetting the past, moving on
Forgiving the ones who do you wrong
Helping those whose road is rough
Praying to the One above
The definition of love

Lori Barba
Apple Creek, OH

Judgement Day

Judgment day is nearing
Of this we're very sure
This world is full of evil
So sinful and impure

Dear friends prepare for judgment
For it is sure to come
If your prepared and waiting
Heaven will be your home

But if your life's not ready
When Jesus does return
You will be cast into the fire
That will forever burn

Jesus gave us clear command
To ever watch and pray
Someday He's coming through the clouds
It could be any day

Rachel Knepp
Montgomery, IN

All That I Ask

Dear Lord, I thank You for all that You've done
To make my life peaceful and free,
And I pray that I'll always merit Your love
And You'll always watch over me.
Temptations are strong in this world of ours
And it takes Your strength to get through.
We would wander alone in the darkness of night
If we couldn't count, Lord, on You.
When I feel downtrodden and weary of heart,
I go to the chapel and pray,
And I feel Your Spirit as You comfort me
And see me on through the day.
Your strength is a staff on which I can lean
And it carries me on my way,
For You are the rock that I will stand on
And the mantle beneath which I will lay.
My life in Your service is what I could ask,
A return that I feel is Your due,
And I'll be doing service for my fellowman
When I show them the right way is You.
If it be my calling, my life will be full,
Thy Word will I spread far and wide.
Then when life is over on this worldly plane,
With You we'll forever abide.

Leroy C. Leach
Lyons, KS

No One Else

No one could ever be
the special things you are to me,
or fill my days, my heart, my world
so very happily.

No one else could comfort me
with just a look or touch,
or make me laugh and help me
to enjoy life half as much.

No one else could be for me
the special kind, perfect blend of a man
who's strong, but also the most
gentle, caring friend.

No one else could understand
and know me like you do.
No one else could be my love—
no one else but you!

Christine Llewellyn
Williamsburg, KY

Bibles

Whether the Bibles are big or small
The Word of God is in them all
They speak of the future and past
The words inside were meant to last.

If we are alone and get lost someday
The Bible will show us the way
All we have to do is open the Bible wide
And all the directions are inside.

Someday the Bible will become
A map for all to see
And guide us forevermore
To Heaven's front door.

Rueben R. Lesser
Hot Springs, SD

Call Me a Comma Lover

I give to you, my students, the gift of commas—
The key does not wear out.
The streets run rampant with ink available for commas;
Do not fear a shortage.
Commas give us a chance to pause in a harried world,
To ignore frenetic timetables,
To inhale deeply, to feel for a vibration of consciousness.
Newspapers and magazines cut them more and more often,
And so do we, because
In a world of ten-foot ceilings, Hummers,
Muffins the size of babies' heads, stilettoes,
We do not have time to pause. They are so small
Because space means money
And how dare we forget the importance of profit?
They do not stop like periods.
They do not drift into nothingness, as do ellipses . . .
Or rush, like dashes—
Or even shout like exclamation points or leave us hanging,
Like question marks.
Instead, they whisper, "Hesitate, think, ponder,
Take note of the world among commas.
Is this what you want to do with your life at this time?"
I want to live in a cave with commas.
Perhaps a friend will drop by so we can talk about
What occurs between the commas.
His hand curves around mine.
Our commas fit together.
I wish I were a comma,
Small, curved, unobtrusive,
Seemingly insignificant, yet purposeful, a wisp on the way,
A yield before the next notion, perhaps reconsidering direction.

Bess Lovec
Billings, MT

Sailor Boy

I was a sailor boy
A few years ago.
Sailed the South Pacific.
Fought a hardy foe.
Still in my teens,
Unforgettable years.
When I think about them,
My heart thumps with fear.
Time and again, my shipmates
Fought a gallant fight.
Foe returned our fire.
'Twas no end in sight.
Several times, we got hit.
Sailor boys were killed.
Ghastly sight to behold
Of blood being spilled.
Strong our will to win.
Never did we retreat.
Our foe turned tail.
Fled, for they were beat.
Sailor boys, sailor boys,
Those buried at sea.
America salutes you,
Loves you, eternally.

Victor E. Legaspi
Calexico, CA

Fire and Rain

I remember living in the Hell-like heat,
The wet, muggy smell in the air,
The feeling that everything is sticky and gross,
The scent of rain soon to come.

I remember how it rained every day,
Every day at about dinner time,
Every day the sound of rushing water,
Every day the roar of distant thunder.

I remember the massive hurricanes,
The rain and hail that destroyed,
The wind that pummeled the buildings,
The aftermath of houses destroyed.

I remember where I am from.
I'm from Florida, and I'm glad to be gone.

Jack McCulloch
Cumming, GA

A Lover's Slumber

I start rubbing your feet and see the pure ecstasy on your face.
I lean into you and enjoy the feel of your embrace.
Our lips meet and the fire ignites.
Warm bodies intertwined to take the sting out of the winter nights.
The feeling is overwhelming and I can't get enough.
Your beard against my bare skin is rough
Like sandpaper rubbing against satin.
The electricity grows, and then fireworks explode
Like the lights of Manhattan.
Together we've collided and out of the sky we descend.
Basking in the glow of our lovemaking
And yet it's not something we can comprehend.
The chill of the night brushes against our wet skin,
Yet we're still warm from within.
A sea of blankets wrapped around us.
We fall asleep in each other's caress.

September McElroy
Shenandoah, IA

. . . And Diapers Too

Every morning, 'long about ten,
I think of things as they might have been—
Of office gossip and computer keys,
And "Miss Smith, will you take a letter, please?"
And here I sit, almost alone,
Spooning cereal into Joan.

Oh, those happy, halcyon, carefree days,
When my shoes were all of the latest craze,
When I shopped and shopped my noon hour through
For a blouse in a certain shade of blue;
Now a prunish purple is more my tone
As I'm spooning cereal into Joan.

But the old sayings are mostly right.
Though my fingernails are now a sight,
A trip to the beauty shop is a treat,
And I haggle the butcher on the price of meat,
Yet I wouldn't trade for the British throne
This spooning cereal into Joan.

Marjorie Matthews
Greenville, TX

Friends

Back in time, I often think
about friends once had that are now a mere blink.
For friends come few and far between,
someone to lean on, to make you smile,
to take your troubles far away for a short while.
There is a specialty amongst friends to
have respect for one another;
what happened to that, I often wonder.
Nowadays, so few take the time
to look at the good and put the rest behind.
Friendship is like a gift that should not be returned,
but as a friend, you will be often heard.
Your kindness, your smile, your laughter, and your cheer
could never replace what once was so dear.

Rhonda L. Moran
Ludington, MI

My Stepfather

You're tough but fair and
taught me many lessons
to make me aware.
Outside your guard is up and
tough is your game,
but inside you're sweet
and fair is your name.
Father to me since I was two,
I learned to appreciate all that you do.
Always there to show you care,
and that inside you're just a sweet teddy bear.
Even since I've left the nest,
I've had to call and learn even more from the best.
Only ever a phone call away,
always there night or day.
Even though we are getting older,
the lessons I've learned
have made me much bolder.
Not afraid to dare or to care,
my father taught me, who is tough, but fair.

Crystal Mayberry
Hershey, PA

The All-American Mom

Up at dawn and on the run,
Get the kids to school,
The baby's off for daycare fun!
On the job all day long,
Where the boss does rule!

After work, they sing a new song,
Johnny to softball, Susie to dance.
A minute for yourself—not a chance!
It's off to the gas pump,
Wow, these prices make me jump!
And my pocketbook leaner.
Oh, yes, I've got to go the dry cleaners!

To the drive-thru for dinner.
Pick up the kids and let them know they are winners!
Home at last to gobble supper,
Homework, bath, a bedtime story,
Say our prayers to give God all glory!
A few tickles and a good night kiss,
You've waited all day for this!
To see them sleeping peaceful is a real upper!

Viola E. McEuin
Broken Bow, OK

Paradise Island

As I'm lying on the beach
Staring at the starry sky
With the sand between my toes
And an incoming tide
The moon is full
And its light is bright
A few puffy clouds
What a beautiful night
Then I gaze into her eyes
And she makes my stomach flutter
Now this is a beauty
Unlike any other
I must be blessed
It is a given
For this woman makes me feel
Like I stepped into heaven
But wait just a minute
What I said was right
Because it happened the moment
She came into my life
With all the joy happiness and laughter
Chris and Jenny will live happily ever after.

Chris Morgan
Rydal, GA

For my beautiful wife, Jennifer, who inspires me. I will always love you—your husband, Chris.

Wedding Vows

Trust and respect are basic and strong.
They are within me for you always,
whether I believe you are right or wrong.
You've nothing to prove to me.
Your decision's your own.
With trust and respect, we've a base; we'll be strong.

I will always encourage creativity
to keep our minds open, our thoughts patterns free.
So that music and art will manifest naturally,
I will always encourage creativity.

And humor, as important as the rising sun
to accompany our lives in work or fun,
for the ability to laugh in hard times or when glum
is as important to our marriage as life's need of the sun.

Most important, there is a always prayer.
You know that I might not agree, but I care.
So with trust and respect as our base
and creativity and humor as our energy,
and prayer as our foundation,
I will accept you as my friend, my lover, and my mate!

Charlotte W. Mraz
Vacaville, CA

After raising two sons by myself and working three jobs, I wrote exactly what I
wanted and needed in a man on June 9, 1990. I started my new life with Joe.
We have had our ups and downs, and after a year, I wrote this. I am fifty-seven
and Joe is sixty. We pray for at least thirty more years of productive living.

Open

Existing for real
Decide for yourself
If this is real or just a tale
Moving through our homes
Roaming through our lives
Orbs, sounds, and such
Not exactly things we can touch
ESP or telepathy
Things of the mind
Maybe another realm beyond
Some don't understand
Although research is done
Notes are taken
Do we really know what we awaken

Michael Lynn McAmis
Greeneville, TN

Remember When

Remember when the Christmas season
Was simple toys and food so pleasin'?
Time has changed our Christmas ways
To busy, expensive shopping days.
Remember when our socks were stuffed
With popcorn balls and apples buffed?
The trees were trimmed with cranberry chains,
And the greatest gift—an electric train.
Remember when the air was ringing
With music, cards, and happy singing,
The radiant face of a happy boy
As he hears the story of Christmas joy?
Today you hang your Christmas sock
While listening to the "Jingle Bell Rock."
Girls want dolls that dance and walk
And a telephone on which to talk.
For the boys, the very latest boon—
An astronaut that lands on the moon;
A color TV of his very own,
And a sign that says "No Parking Zone."
We all eat out our Christmas fare,
Steak, instead of turkey, medium rare.
Yes, remember when the Christmas season
Was simple toys and food so pleasin'?

Rachael C. Mason
Edmond, OK

Woven Thoughts Come Together

Constant motion is known as surf.
Few things in life remain the same.
Relationships change with time; locations, our
Turf.
Inspired wild experiences . . . chances taken . . .
Never tame.

Then a quiet walk along the beach;
Tide's out, driftwood and shells left behind,
Found by me and collected and used to teach.
So many saved, then woven colors, textures in
And out with creativity in mind

Constant motion and squeals of the two-year-old
Brings joy to parents, grandparents, and great-grands.
Sometimes "owies" and cries woven to a
Calmness with a gentle scold.
Hugs and kisses woven in experiences, changes
Made . . . we are all fans.

Bonnie Neuman
Evart, MI

Being a retired art educator, I've become interested in artistic mixed media. My poem, "Woven Thoughts Come Together," is often exhibited with one of my hand-loom weaving wall hangings. I also include a large photo of a granddaughter at the edge of the seashore off Sanibel Island, Florida. I've lived with my husband, James, on a farm in northwestern Michigan for fifty-three years. We have four grown children, eight grandchildren, two great-grandchildren, and eight international exchange students through the years. We have spent winters in Fort Myers, Florida since 1990. I find writing poetry allows expression of thoughts in new ways.

Mowing Grass

I sat upon a housetop
Waiting with a friend
For the passing of a flood
Which seemed to have no end.

I gazed about upon the flood,
Then looked at the water below.
I was amazed at what I saw,
A hat moving to and fro.

I made comment to my friend,
Who smiled a smile of cheer.
"Ignore the hat," he said to me,
"Let it cause no fear."

"That's my dad you see down there,
And though he seems absurd,
When he says he'll do a thing,
He always keeps his word."

"I heard him say just last night
Another day won't pass
That hell so hot nor waters high
Will stop my mowing grass."

Joe Nations
Mount Airy, NC

A Necklace of Peace

I would like to make
A necklace of peace and
Put it around the world,
Connecting every distant shore,
His goodness would reign once more!

It would ever be on display
For all mankind to see.
It would never, ever break,
Each nation clasped in give and take,
Keep promises that they make!

To make a better world,
Spread jeweled rays of good,
Ever so strong in unity.
Friendly binds by a handshake,
Keepsakes would be all they'd make!

It would sparkle everywhere at night,
Light up, eradicate war's gloom!
It would be priceless as the Trinity.
It would encircle you and me,
Last for all eternity!

Mildred Nelson
Greeneville, TN

Hands of Comfort

I heard the hands of comfort coming down the hall.
It was Mother coming to wipe my sweaty brow and bring me food.
Her hands were thin not from age, but from trying to save my
three-year-old sister from the flames that had engulfed her.
I never saw my sister, but I always knew her from my mother's hands.
Often those hands gave perms to the girls in the country when her
hands were well enough to curl, for the perm solution created pain,
yet those hands continued to give to her family and friends
without complaint.
Hands of comfort come in many different sizes and forms.
Hands that reach out to take yours in greetings of joy
or times of sorrow; the touch of a hand brings comfort one can afford.
Hands could be from a baby to the oldest, it doesn't matter the age.
The thing that does matter is what is done with those hands.
A young child may take both of their hands and place them on
each side of your face to get your attention
or just a pleasant embrace.
Just a hand upon a lad's head makes him feel special and he will grin.
A hand upon a shoulder brings fellowship much closer for a friend.
Have you given thought of how important your hands are?
Have you thought about how valuable your hands are?
Comfort through your hands today is more than money can buy.
Your hands of comfort are worth living for, so don't be discouraged.
There is much for you to do. Just reach out with your hands and
express your love, even if words do not come.
The comfort of hands is never forgotten,
so don't forget to lend your hands.

Carolyn Norris
Benton, AR

Time

Days melt away
into years
bringing smiles
bearing tears
First it's a crib
then a doll
A young man
comes to call
Puppies and kites
and old tennis shoes
Diaries and lipstick
and dresses of blue
Church in the afternoon
saying "I do"
Satin and lace
pink roses too
Now they have babes
of their own
Someday they too
will be grown
I would have
walked slower
talked less
listened more
had I known
more about time.

Lorelle Pederson
Spokane, WA

All Between Sixty-Two
and Seventy-Two Degrees

Second by parsing second
I see most of it in syllables.
Yes, I've gone into poetry—

No story lines, just moods
Of shifting and conflation.
My concocted reveries mangle

Any spectrum in bursts of opposites.
My wife watches TV dramas—
She has gone to *Hill Street Blues*,

China Beach, *The West Wing*, ER
Where there are plots and people.
Recently I pulled a ligament

On the back of my hand while giving
The finger to my closet door,
But I have my one-inch stack of poems.

Now I'm in my fungus years.
I set rat traps and gopher traps
That never snap.

Art Palfrey
Leucadia, CA

Fitch

My name is Fitch.
At school they said it rhymed with "b****."
I did not understand,
but still took a stand.

Mom and Dad had eight of us.
Now there are three of us.

Helen, Bonnie, and Lib are gone.
Jack and Mike are gone.
Jim, Sam, and I are still here.
but life is slipping away from here.

After I married Butch, he said, "How do you spell Fitch?
Is that with a b, as in 'b****'?"
I said yes to my husband Butch.

Don't get me wrong,
the name Fitch is strong.
You see, we have all believed in God
and that is good.

Linda Fitch Greene
Shelby, NC

My Friend

Friends come and go as the years go by.
I see friends I had in school,
but to my surprise, they just walk on by
without saying
"Hi! How are you?"
But you, see my friend,
you are there for the good times and bad times.
My friend, you hold a place in my heart.
We laugh together and we cry together.
My friend, you never lost
touch with me, even when I was miles away.
Now since we are just
blocks away, my friend,
the sparks between us
still light up after all these years.
My friend, you see,
we come to know each other
like a book with no ending,
just more chapters to be written.

Tara Gerstenberg
Summit Hill, PA

I started to write poetry in 1991 when I was a freshman in school. My inspiration for this poem came from working with the public. I see many people I went to school with, but nobody stops to talk. Nobody has time unless it's on the computer, but this one person I know has been there for everything and still is. This friend never lost touch with me. Now we have been neighbors for many years and our friendship keeps growing stronger as the days go by.

Nanna Banana's Ice Cream

Welcome, big and little shavers, to my house of many flavors!
Here you'll find the greatest ice cream in the world!
Before you say you'll buy it, why not come on up and try it?
We've got something here for every boy and girl!
We've got peanut butter brickle, peachy apple, lemon prickle,
Chocolate-coconut-banana-pink surprise!
Blueberry-orange spicy, cherry-nilla-berry icey,
We invent new flavors right before your eyes!
Chocolate-hazelnut-raspberry, peppermint and cherry merry,
Yummy butterscotch and marshmallow supreme,
Pow-pow punch and buttercrunchy, lime 'n' almond mango munchy,
We can satisfy your wildest ice cream dream!
Java-fudgy-cocoa-toffee, mocha-buzzy-wuzzy coffee,
Bubble gummy-taffy-pineapple parfait.
Calling all you flavor-cravers, do yourself a big fat favor—
Visit Nanna's crazy ice cream shop today!

Ellen Godfrey
Foxborough, MA

Don't Forget to Think About Me

When I am away from you,
all I do is think all the time.
How wonderful it could be if you were mine.
It's easy to understand how you could fall so hard.
You're not the only one who's been
taken in and torn apart.
I'm scared, lonely, and the nights grow cold.
Without you, I have no one to hold.
I have been alone way too long,
who knows anymore what's right or wrong.
The things I dream of every single night
with you in my life is the only thing
that feels right.
I don't want to fall and hurt myself.
I want to be there for you and no one else.
Way up in the sky, the first star I see.
Please don't forget to think about me.

Wanda Franklin
Halifax, VA

My Farewell

My spirit has ascended
To my precious Lord on high.
I've gone to claim my mansion
In my home beyond the sky!
I'll be waiting with my Savior
To be with you all again.
Oh, what joy there'll be in Heaven,
Where there's no more pain or sin!
No more worries, hurts, or hard times,
No more trying to survive.
No more sadness, tears, or heartaches,
No more doubts or fears or strife,
Only praise and pure contentment
With our awesome, blessed Lord.
I'm so glad that I have trusted
In His holy Living Word!
For me, this journey's over,
But I leave you with this prayer
That you'll all accept the Savior
So we'll be together there!
I love you all!

Virginia DeGroat
Lapeer, MI

Endless Love

Love is an endless line,
A vow that is accepted and given,
An all-encompassing mood between two.
It's an unspoken word, a loving glance.
A priceless gift none other to compare.
Love is even the feeling of despair.
To find your mate and share your life,
Always keep God and His might.
Yes, for two can build and multiply,
But with God as your copilot,
No destination's too far to fly!
Never let the line be broken
For lack of an apology unspoken.
Begin each day as if anew,
And then love is always within you!
Your spouse is the most precious gift,
Who, when protected, cuddled, and nurtured,
Will be the first and last of your thoughts
In your life of endless love!

Mary Lou Jackson
Groves, TX

Damn Auto

My auto don't wanna go
I shine her for the show
She got the starting spark
The engine she no bark
My auto still no go
My auto don't wanna go
My auto oughta go
I take the money from the bank
To put the gas into the tank
My auto still no go
My auto don't wanna go
I can't afford a tow
The oil she in the pan
The belt she on the fan
My auto still no go
My auto don't wanna go
I shout and steam and blow
The seat belt she is fastened
The door lock she is snappin'
My auto still no go
My auto don't wanna go
Warning light she do not glow
I turn the key in anticipation
Then I frown in desperation
My auto still no go

William C. Bateman
Whispering Pines, NC

Little Things

It's little things that make my day,
like a grandchild's big warm smile
that makes my anguish, go away
and makes everything worthwhile.

It's little things like great big hugs
that mean so much to me,
and life just fits together
like a ship out on the sea.

Like sitting on your front porch,
watching everyone walk by,
or watching a bald eagle
flying high up in the sky.

Strolling through the woods
on a real warm summer day,
watching all the animals
while they're eating or at play.

Sitting with a loved one,
how much better could it be.
Being blessed with little things
means the whole world to me.

Donald L. Waugh
Oswego, NY

Change

It is a part of life.
We may see things differently than before.
Change can give us new adventures.
We can try something that we never did before.
We can make new discoveries about ourselves.
If we make changes, it can help us grow for the better.
We may be a better person because of it.
Change can be good.

Raymond Barszewski
Sunderland, MA

I came from a loving family that encouraged me to do my best. My family is Polish. I work as a janitor. I have taken courses in writing in college. I have read books on writing and on poetry. People have said they like my poetry, so I am writing more. The poem, "Change," was inspired by changes I have made in my life. God is the center of my life, more now. Also, I do what is needed to have a healthy lifestyle.

Outdoors

The gentle breeze makes my hair blow,
Noisy lawnmower runs steady and slow.
Mind wanders dazing into cloudless blue sky,
Dreaming what it is like so high.

Leaves tickle one another on the tree,
Doing all this as I sip my Celestial tea.

Some cars go whizzing by
As passengers wave hi.
Radio broadcasts the Cardinals baseball game,
Whoever wins, we will all still be the same.

In the far-off distance, I see the hills,
Knowing the river below will not stay still.

The sun shines radiantly
To dry up the inches of rain immediately.
Blades of grass lean left and right,
It may be windy enough for my kite.

Linda Becker
Union, MO

Don't Tell Me You Have Nothing to Do!

How can you say you have nothing to do?
How can you tell me that you are bored, too?
Why, when I was your age,
I'd get lost in a page
While reading a good book or two.
How can you sit there just moping around
When everywhere treasure just waits to be found!
There's adventure and sports,
And romance of all sorts,
And the heroes and villains abound.
How can you say that you don't like to read?
If you won't try, you may never succeed
In fulfilling your goal
Of outwitting the troll
And rescuing damsels in need.
How can I urge you to try a good book?
How can you pass up the chance for a look
At the dragons of old
And the wagons of gold
Or the brews which some witches will cook?
How do the tales of real people move you?
Read with your heart and you'll find that it's true
That we can live our days
In miraculous ways,
So don't say you've nothing to do!

Carol Lee Bellairs
Clarinda, IA

Window Seat Over Reno, Nevada

The plane ascends—
A late dusk burns the sky in crimson and azure.
Shimmering sagebrush Sierras cascade
Over a frivolous fountain between glacier
And salt lakes: the Truckee River. Snow-capped peaks
Of Mt. Rose's summit are riddles to the valley,
As the melted mountain powder drizzles
Into the Great Basin waterway.

The twinkle twilight pulsates
Amidst the thin transient atmosphere,
Spreading the city's complexion
Along its desolate sun-drenched meadows.
The streets crowed—with more light
And more elements than the periodic table.

Harry Baker
Sparks, NV

Broken

Boom! Bang! Cannons and guns firing everywhere
Enter the war, if you dare
"I want you" says Uncle Sam
How in the world could he want me?
I mean, what do I do, leave my family?
All my wife can do is make razors
This is all so new, yet entirely major
The Japanese-Americans sent to interment camps
It's like a person who just got a cramp
With everything changing both here and there
I go out to war, better start my prayer
I bet back home, my wife's Rosie the Riveter
And my kids are collecting wires and tires
To help make supplies and other things we need
He's coming closer to me, I think I just peed
I hear my heart beating—boom!
I just shot him dead and right in the head!
Now I journey back home, it's been three years
And as I get closer, my eyes fill with tears
I am actually getting kind of scared
My country's one of the few not attacked
But soon we're all going to get back on track
No more war, that would be nice
If we were friends, like two little mice
Oh, look over there, it's Pearl Harbor
What type of birds are those in the sky?
Boom! Bang! Excuse me while I die

Makaela Bailey
Sweetwater, TN

My Daily Prayer

Heavenly Father
I thank You for this day
Teach me how to live
Teach me how to pray.
Take away all my fears
That are with me every day
And give me the courage and the strength
To guide me all the way.
Let me not be so selfish
Let me not be so cruel
Pour Your love into my heart
To be my golden rule.
Let my faith be very strong
To carry out Your deeds
And not to think of mine alone
But someone else's needs.
Let my heart be opened wide
To let Your love pour in
To keep away all temptations
That cause us all to sin.
Melt the ice around my heart
And warm it with Your hands
That I may be a better person
To follow Your commands.

Joann Balistrieri
Pittsburgh, PA

Untitled

When I go to my grandpa's house
There's lots of things to do
I greet my grandpa so way up high
A hug and a kiss for you.
I can sit on his lap and
He'll tell me a story of days
Before I was born, a few secrets
About my dad, or of a long-
Ago war that we once had.
Maybe we'll go out into the yard
Play with a ball or fly a kite
Grandpa's with me, he's right here
To help and watch, in full view
From his wheelchair.
It doesn't matter that he sits
To watch me play, as long as he's there
For he's as tall as any grandpa
And he's mine, shiny wheels and all!

Donna Brummage
Massillon, OH

Summer Night

As I lay in the dark,
lightning bugs flit over my head.
As the stars sing their songs,
I consider the grass my bed.
I gaze up in wonder,
a cool breeze swimming in the grass
that ripples my clothes and
whispers words said in the past.
"Be quiet, my dear child,"
says a gentle, calm voice to me.
"Do not be afraid,
for I will not let harm come to thee."
My whole being agrees.
Slowly, the voice fades away.
I stare at the heavens,
and the sun tells of a new day.
Then suddenly, I start.
I sit bolt upright in my bed.
It was only a dream,
still I hear the words that were said.
I close my tired eyes
as I hear the loud whir of birds,
and I heave a large sigh
and think about those lovely words.

Aimee Becker
Bloomsburg, PA

Early Spring

The early morning air is crisp and clear.
From my rocking chair on the deck,
I can hear a chickadee calling out for a mate.
A pair of quacking mallards fly overhead.
The songbirds are just arriving at the feeders—
chickadees, juncos, finches, a nuthatch.
Two cowbirds watch from afar, fearing my presence.
The call of a red-winged blackbird pierces through the air.
A muskrat glides slowly along the edge of the pond,
making ripples in the otherwise glass like surface.
An occasional truck can be heard on a nearby road,
the only reminder that I'm not alone in the wilderness.
It's May first. The leaves are just budding on the maples
in the Green Mountains of Vermont.
One small pile of snow remains in a shady spot, surely to melt today.
In a world of turmoil, this is peace.

Susan Armstrong
Woodford, VT

Feeding . . . the Young and the Old

I fix some pancakes for my two-year-old grandson.
He asks me to cut them up for him and pour on the syrup.
"Grammy," he says, "help me," and I do.
He drops pieces of pancakes on the floor
and smears syrup all over his hands.
When he finishes, I chase him around the kitchen
trying to wipe his hands and face.
This is a difficult task, this feeding a two-year-old.
Three hours later, I travel to the nursing home.
The food is already prepared for my ninety-one-year-old mother,
so I don't have to cook for her.
I sit next to her at the table and ask her what she wants to eat.
I spear some turkey and dressing with her fork and hand it to her.
She looks at it questioningly and then looks at me.
I nod to her and tell her to go ahead and put it in her mouth.
She does and then we repeat the same procedure over and over.
She spills some food on her clothing protector
and on her lap, but we ignore it.
When she finishes, after a considerable amount of time,
she sits quietly while I wipe her hands and face.
Feeding a ninety-one-year-old is a difficult task as well,
but for very different reasons.

Mary L. Anthony
Jacksonville, IL

Reflections of a Beautiful Woman

Beautiful woman looking back at me from the mirror that I hold in my hand, what is it that you see in the eyes that gaze at you countless times in any given day?

Do you see a child playing, so full of life, or a woman in her youth who has just found true love?

Mirror of my image, mirror that I hold in my hand beckons memories of days gone by, days filled with play, laughter, happy days full of joy, wondrous times of long ago.

Beautiful woman gazing back at me, softly spoken, whispering, listening to what I have to say.
Unspoken words left unsaid, many times I've failed to tell you just how beautiful you are.

Maria C. Appelzoller
Albuquerque, NM

Flag Waving

Red is for the blood on your shoulder.
White is for the paint on your skin.
Blue is for the night that is colder.
Stars dot the sky on the glen.
You wave for attention of others.
Your garments do flutter in breeze.
You protect all the children and mothers.
You sent younger men overseas.
We all raise our hands to solute you,
Watching your emblem for all.
Your men are the proud and the few,
But all of them answer your call.
Our country is home to money and jewels,
But wealth doesn't matter at all.
You value courage and tools
So your freedom won't waver or fall.
We want your faith and justice
To help us stand tall, flag waving.

Bonnie Barnett
Osceola, AR

Grandma's House

My grandma reminds me of an old mother hen.
She had so many children, they added up to ten.
All day long she sat in her rocking chair,
Reminiscing about how she always tried to be honest
And fair.
Her days became quite lonely and drab.
She felt sometimes like an old crab.
Soon as she would see a grandchild coming in the
Door,
She would give them a big hug and much more.
Hurriedly out to the kitchen she flew,
Busy baking dozens of cookies and tea she would brew.
When a grandchild happened to spend the night.
The scary stories she would tell could be quite a
Fright.
On Sunday morning around the piano, we would
Gather,
Sing hymns and giving thanks to God for all things
That mattered.

Delores Benge
Mt. Pleasant, IA

Suddenly . . .

I recall when I was young, the days were without end,
The raindrops never seemed to stop, the road never bend.
And then, as I grew older, the days of endless school,
The waiting for the recess . . . was this to be the rule?

I remember seeing vast blue sky, with fleecy clouds above
Perhaps it was the time to fashion thoughts of love?
But these were quickly chased from mind,
The time was spent in daily grind . . . an endless grind.

And then, the days seemed shorter, the minutes flit by.
I had no reason to suspect the reason why.
Long forgot the school, the vast blue sky was gone.
I had gotten older . . . eternity was yon.

And then one day God called me . . . suddenly.

Poet Cavanaugh
Herminie, PA

The Difference

I used to do what I had to do
In order to survive.

Today I do what I love to do
And truly feel alive.

There have been many times in my life
When my emotions felt at a low,
Yet I had to get "outta" myself
And give of myself
To get my life back in tow.

Always be a good listener to others
As you pass them on your way.
Their load may be heavy on any given day.
You may be the chosen one
That makes the difference,
So listen carefully to the words they have to say.

Our load becomes lighter
With love in your heart
When we greet each day with a smile.
Truly know within, we're all in this big world
For only a little while.

Jo Ann Boggs Cordova
Hesperia, CA

Called Me

I know what you dreamt last night alone in your cold, hard bed.
You dreamt you were born to endless fright
and wished to rather be dead.
You had night visions of despair and pain,
the lingering scents of woe.
Caring much, writhing in blood, slain, knowing not to stay or go.
All of our humanity has been replaced by vanity,
which led to our insanity.
I know what was on your mind as you lay asleep.
You were thinking of a crime and a heart to keep.
Propping it up on your bedside for only you to see.
Your darkest secrets will abide in the heart called me.
What has caused all the blind? And the ones who cannot hear?
For sight lost, looking will they find all hope put out by fear?
Give unto me your weakest link, for they will be put in chains.
Put in the ocean to swim or sink, and the world will call it a game.
Having said that give me your best so they can be set free.
They will soon be laid to rest by a gentle hand called me.

Tia Cowger
Wheeler, IL

I live in a very rural community, otherwise known as the middle of nowhere.
My friends and family are awesome and super-supportive. I write what I feel.
If I'm happy, my prose sounds happy, and if I'm sad, it's sad. Anyway, thanks
and God bless.

My Grandson

I'm a regular mom
Just trying to stay calm.
Never had a son.
My grand is lots of fun.
Before it gets dark,
We go to a nearby park.
My four-year-old grandson is so dear,
It's going to kill me when he leaves here.
I thought we would never be apart,
I'm losing it, it's breaking my heart.
Far away to another state
Is something I just hate.
So they can leave me, I will not help them pack,
I just want them to come back.
I love my grand, he's so small,
Every day hoping they will call.
He loves to play with my hair,
Who will take my place, I can't bear.
I know he's not in Rome,
I want my grand to come home.

Janet Callahan
Lumberton, NC

Untitled

Trees, stately sentinels, guard castle
walls, holding secure these
hallowed halls.
Old wisdom, the wood, through millennia
will lead, grants the earth new
birth through seed.
Cragged, skyward, twisted, yet true,
bows to only God under the blue.
For warmth, shelter, creatures lead to
the stands,
toiled weathered men, axes, saws in hand
take from the sentinels only
the best—then take rest.
Old wisdom, the wood, through millennia
will lead, grants the earth new birth
through seed.

Daniel Casey
Garden Prairie, IL

So Why Worry?

Sometimes we need to show that we care.
Usually what helps the most is if we can just be there.
Your children love you and need your help, I'd say,
Especially if someone is sick or has too many bills to pay.
We worry about their struggles and hope they learn from you,
But we all have to learn for ourselves—the best that we can do.
If you think about it, worry is sorta like a rocking chair—
If gives you something to do, but doesn't get you anywhere.
So why worry?

Zelma I. Drake
Beatrice, NE

Sweat Lodge Woman

Naked in the steamy dark,
Fanning flame with feather,
Chanting.

Breathing in the steamy dark,
Water poured on red hot stones,
Singing.

Rhythms in the steamy dark,
Purging ills from mind and body,
Praying.

Charles W. Bailey
Venice, CA

The Rose

For me, you are a hybrid of the bright yellow and pure white roses,
yellow for friendship, white for hope, and the rose
because it has petals as soft as your kindness,
a fragrance as intoxicating as your smile,
and the thorns,
which are your protection against those who might hurt you
I want you to know that I am a rose, too,
a hybrid of the bright yellow and musty grey roses,
yellow for friendship,
grey for the darkness of the past that I haven't yet forgotten
I have never blossomed!
My beauty has never been seen and
my fragrance has not escaped from its prison
Like you, I, too have thorns, so many and so large
that the precious yellow and grey rose is concealed
but . . .
rose can tear through the wall of thorns and soon
she will gain the courage to fight her way out!
Her petals will be shed in that battle
and what will emerge will be a soft, yellow dandelion
Yellow because I hope we are still friends after that battle,
and I will be a dandelion
for my true beauty will not be seen on the surface,
my fragrance will be shared with only one,
and I shall have no thorns!

Rachel E. Goldstein
New Windsor, NY

Under the Influence

Of wine, of beer,
of nothing at all.
I still don't think clear.

Of cocaine, of weed,
which helps in times of need,
but offer no direction of which I desperately need.

Of depression, of anger,
to myself I'm a stranger.
Of love, of hate . . .
I still don't think straight.

Of family, of friends,
no clue where it ends.
Of insomnia and irritability,
don't want to address basic responsibilities.
Of lust and allure,
still compare myself to the next him or her.

Under the influence of you,
and not sure what to do . . .
but under the influence of me
can almost be guaranteed . . .

a dangerous place to be.

Jaime Smith
Avon Lake, OH

Friday Night

The acrid aftertaste of citrus gum
and last night's eggplant parmigiana
is enough to wake me up at two a.m.
to a sweaty leather couch
I do not recognize
and throbbing toes,
I cannot remember why.
I remember only
the screaming,
the bitter words,
the bitter, bitter cold.
I wish you would have hugged me sooner,
but I forgive you.
I'll forgive you anything
if you just come back to bed with me.
Quit staring out the window
at the distant stars.
Two a.m. is not the time for fairy tales,
and you are my Prince Charming.
So come back,
I need a kiss good night,
or maybe one good morning,
or both;
I can't decide.
I only want to wake up again
with the taste of you on my lips.

Loren Oumarova
Brooklyn, NY

Heaven's Gate

I've heard men say each passing day
A phrase that puzzles me
For it does show that they don't know
The way things ought to be
And though they strived and even tried
To toss their guilt away
They still can't seem to wake their dream
For this is what they say
If but I knew which way was true
Which life's crossroad to take
Then I could choose and never lose
My way to Heaven's gate
But as they grope in search of hope
To find that golden sky
They know the task but still they ask
Where does the answer lie
If only they would stop and pray
For guidance from the Lord
Then follow next the holy text
Therein they'd find reward
For all who seek the strong or weak
Will always find the truth
If search they will with all their skill
The scriptures wrath and Ruth

Yonge K. Sage
Bullard, TX

A Soldier's Widow

Two oceans we were
Vast and mighty, the same
Massive in amour, magnificent to adore
Until the sands of time eroded the shore
Now we are nothing more
Shoulder to shoulder until justice was done

Together, we were one
Shoulder to shoulder until love was won
Now we are none

With only metals to have and a flag to hold
Neither fills the emptiness within my soul
My heart is so weak while the days and nights are eloign
With embers still warm
But for how long

Alfonzer Jones
Durham, NC

Eternal Maine

In spring the trees unfold their buds
In delicate lacy fronds,
But the stately pines are already green
Protecting the trout-filled ponds.

Summertime brings magic walks
In forests of varied greens,
All trees blended together—
But the scent of the pines, so clean.

The richness of autumn colors
Is breathtaking to behold
With the backdrop of the verdant green—
Maine's pines those colors hold.

And then in the stillness of winter
With all under blanket of white,
The stately pine, like a sentinel,
Stands green through the winter night.

Maine's sentinel and its symbol
Of strength and simplicity,
The sentinel and the symbol
Of Maine's eternity.

Elaine Peverly
Kittery, ME

Farewell to the Unknown

As I lie still and wait my soul to rest
Unwelcome darkness pulling down my eyelids
In double spaces, horizontal in my chest
A beating heart is melting sorrow's acids
Surrounded by cocoons with handsome faces
As shadows on the walls paint tentacles of squids
You tear the curtains quietly from spaces
I feel I've lost you when we have never met
The dance, the passion, lips and those caresses—
That hurricane, that heat, that rain I won't forget
A silent movie ending with some shutters locked
Unwanted shelter—I'll always regret

As I must die a while and go to unknown places
Farewell, immortal love, I bow to you with graces.

Iolanda Scripca
Vista, CA

Untitled

My heart—it wails and I'm half-insane
as I hear the screams of my little boy's pain.
The river of tears falls to the bed
as he clutches me closer to his tortured little head.
The world is gone, my worries are none
as I pray to my God for the pain in my son.
I want back the smile, the laughs, and the joy
that are buried within my sick little boy.
The moments of peace, they seem very few,
as if they were strangers, not something I knew.
But come, they do, with a welcome relief
to give a small break, then back to the grief.
The waiting on tests and the words of the doc,
they weigh very heavy like the hour of the clock.
The hours that come and the hours that go—
why do they seem to go oh, so slow?
The day turns to night and back into day,
they're just pictures in a window so very far away.
I guess these are the days that we all must face
to continue our world, our own human race.
Be they boy or girl, Black or White,
something within us helps them to fight.
As parents, we ask our God up above
to let them get well with the help of our love.

I love you, Mike . . . Dad.

Ken Herholz
Nokomis, FL

Ode to Sufferings Past

Through life's toil and trouble the march of suffering endures
With countless escapes, we cannot for long avoid its clutches
But for the passage of time and memory lapses, we survive
To realize with maturity the limited reach it has into our lives
As guides to self-understanding and mid-course corrections
In greater equanimity and happiness, we live a more fulfilled life
Yet in mindfulness as impartial observers, suffering recedes
Without being lured by its temptation, it cannot long survive
As if to shine a light, revealing suffering with no lasting hold
And now the most stubborn of feelings are left in the cold
Yet determined to lessen the burden of our suffering
How fortunate to possess the power of proactive positive thinking
As if to practice viewing the glass half-full, not half-empty
And now seeing the most positive outcomes to restore sanity
Yet remains more to be done to release suffering's grasp
Realizing that our ego attachment binds us to suffering's way
As a monkey not letting go while pulling fruit from narrow-necked jar
And now with detachment to that which we cannot bar
Yet further to decrease suffering by undermining its basis—ego
To know all that changes within us has for so long defined us
As if peacefully anchored rather than conforming to ocean's wave
And not to react to situations realizing we are not our ego's slave
Yet finally we continue, determined not to slip back into suffering
Armed with mindfulness, positive thinking, detachment,
And ego awareness
Now in greater equanimity and happiness we can live, yet not rest
Until fulfillment is attained in lasting bliss per our quest.

Dave Schmidt
San Diego, CA

Memories of a Special Granddaughter

It was in November on the twenty-first day.
The wind blew cold, the sky was gray.
Came a gift from God, as you would prove to be
To those who knew you, especially your family.
We sang in the bathtub and enunciated Papaw,
But we'd have to admit we missed you calling him "Cacaw."
As we dressed you for church and I braided your hair,
I thanked God in Heaven for your mom and your dad
Who were willing to share.
Your hugs you gave freely to young and to old.
To me and to Papaw, they were worth more than gold.
As you grew, we talked about the Bible, how to study on your own,
And that mortals don't become angels when we pass on.
We talked about the beauty of a radiant twilight
And about Heaven; what it would be like.
The last thing you asked me for was an "I Can Only Imagine" CD.
No one could have guessed how soon His face you would see.
You dreamed that you died that very week.
Then came the accident of which we can hardly speak.
When the shoes you were wearing on the day that you passed
At your funeral were brought out, your youth pastor asked,
"Who's ready to fill them, to take up her place?
Who's willing to go and to run her race?"
We know where you are, and we'll soon be there too.
Till then, we will cherish sweet memories of you.

Dianne L. Morrison
Taylorsville, NC

In the world's eyes, Brittany was my step granddaughter. To me, she was my daughter. From the time Brittany was three weeks old, we began keeping her every weekend, from Friday afternoon until Sunday afternoon. On Sundays, we took her to church with us. There was an instant bond to Papaw and me, and us to her, beyond explanation. When she died at age fifteen, that bond never waned.

Don't Treat Us Old

I know we're older than you
And your respect for our age, I admire,
But remember, someday, you'll be our age
And someone's help you may require
Put yourself in our place
Just for a while, and see what it feels like
When people look at you
And just smile
So when you think we need help
At kind of a strenuous task,
Don't take that away,
Just wait until we ask.

Mable Long
Columbia, KY

I can go to the store, and if I'm going to pick up a twenty to twenty-five-pound bag of something, someone says, "I can get that for you," and it makes me feel kind of helpless. When we can and while we can, let us do what we can, thus the poem, "Don't Treat Us Old."

Heartfelt

I felt the knock upon the door
of my sick heart ... and then the sore
inflections of the steely knife
that moved and quickly took my life.

The prick and tug of needle's knot ...
then soothing rush of blood held, caught
by gentle hands that knew my soul
before the moment it was whole.

The knowledge of my heart's design ...
its constant beat, expressly mine,
become the rhythm I will know
while dreaming, waking ... through life I go.

Until the time when mends won't keep
my heart from breaking, then I'll sleep
without the dread of pain or fear ...
with rhythm only God can hear.

Barbara Ann Beswick
Sebring, FL

Writing poetry is what I do to take a break from searching for a publisher for my first novel, *The Sensuous Disciple*. It is very difficult to publish fiction, even though I've been published by big names in nonfiction. I was inspired to write this poem when a friend of my husband called to say that he had just undergone major heart surgery and was feeling fine. He was in his late seventies and older than my husband at the time. We were shocked and thrilled with the news that he made it through. John is still active today.

Wood Spirits

Come with me to the wooden palace
where mystery dwells 'tween rock and crevice.
'Tis filled with bushes and stately trees,
winding trails, squirrels, and buzzing bees.
Come! Enter the gateless passage
and read Mother Nature's message!
See parading elves and beckoning gnomes
hopping and skipping from stone to stone.
Follow them into deep, shadowy corners where
leprechauns dwell by the still, dark waters.
There, in mirthful silence, they await
a wandering artist to seal their fate.
He will chip away at pine, elm, or oak
to create new images with skillful strokes.
Soon, ancestral images evolve once more to a renewed life,
recalled by a sculptor and his knife.

Virginia Shaheen
North Reading, MA

After the Weeping

After the weeping reality abounds
The children are gone where the angels are found
God will heal the hurt but
The pain will remain forever in this
City where so many have been slain

The hand that spun this wrath will
Forever burn in Hell as the weeping
Souls cry out, justice, justice,
Justice, must prevail

The verdict is sealed
And the sentence is giv'n
Tears fill the eyes of mothers' hearts grieving
Another soul will perish but will this stop
The pain in this great city of love
The weeping goes on
But now the healing begins

Ralph C. Prescott
Gibson, GA

Reflections on an Old-Time Christmas

The caroling and the toll of bells
The smell of plum pudding and gingerbread
The aroma of a fresh cut tree
These things bring pleasant memories to me

The silent mantel of falling snow
Decorates the landscape of my mind

A sleigh and the clip-clop of shoes on ice
Are visions of the past

The glow of a yule log and hot glug
Warms my spirit and my heart

May you recall these things and more
An old-time Christmas to you all

Richard Kenney
Coronado, CA

Untitled

There once was a turkey
Named Sue,
Who was so very, very blue.
She wanted to get thinner
So she wouldn't get invited
To dinner
And end up in somebody's stew.

Norma J. Miller
Keokuk, IA

The Present Birthday

A number on the calendar,
What does that indicate?
That we are one year older
And life is getting late.
That years are piling up
In the corner of our heart,
And memories once stored
Are beginning to depart.
We treasure every birthday
Not really getting old!
Just storing more memories
Like jewels and precious gold.

Mary Jane Schafer
Lemont, IL

Inside My Heart

Inside my heart contains a lot of love
It comes from the Lord sent from above
It tells of love past and present too
It tells, in fact, words from me to you.

My brother, one I love
Always have, always will
In my heart still.

You have grown and gone
Your separate way
My love still remains
Keep close to me, dear brother
I need you very much
Your strength, your comfort, things that are such.

Know that my love is for real
Never doubt it's how I feel
We will be close together even while apart
We will be close together forever in my heart
To love you more each and every day
Precious words we can always say.

Brother of mine, from the very start
A love burns brightly
Inside my heart.

Althea Lani
Ely, NV

I am a married mother of three children. I've written poems since age thirteen.
My poetry comes to me naturally and this was inspired by events during my
lifetime.

The Young Doctor's Journey

In this young doctor's journeying, as he hungered and searched for truth and answers to so much pain, sorrow, and suffering, he came upon the Great Physician, who had been waiting for him for such a long, long time.

The young doctor said, "I am looking for answers, Lord. Please tell me what I need to know. Tell me what I can do!"

"So many questions and so many answers, and you have them all in me." Then He smiled and reached out His hand and said, "Come and let us visit and walk, my child."

The young doctor took hold and they began to walk and talk for what seemed a long, long while. The two physicians meshed. The two worlds, the two hearts, the two lives came together, mind, body, heart and soul. The young doctor was to return with his life, at last made whole. Oh, he knew not all the answers to do everything, and perfect he would not be; perfection was not his quest, you see, but he now had found the strength and heart and courage to do all he could, and he knew he always would. He found God's plan! Simply to do whatever you can, to love and to care, to heal, comfort, to just be there and to reach out in prayer.

They at last returned to where they first met, where their roads crossed; now each with one mind and one accord, each with their own part to do, yet together as they went their different ways, the Lord, the Great Physician, spoke once more to the young doctor in deep love. "My son, I am never far from you. I am never far away. Call me, seek me, for I am ever with you, always and forever until the end of days!

Linda Gayle Crosby
Darien, GA

I actually have been writing poetry since I was a very young woman. I wrote this poem as a tribute to my oncologist. I am a six-month breast cancer survivor and I wanted to honor Dr. Anthony Moran, for whom I have great admiration and respect. He is not just my doctor, he is my friend—he cares, which is a rarity today. I've been a widow for seventeen years, and I live alone. I am a woman who loves the Lord and life. I try to live each day in appreciation of life and celebrate it. I've been writing for years. I have about thirty journals to leave my sons. I've been through a lot of health problems, but the magic word is "through." We go through and come out on the other side, and I've learned to count my "haves" instead of my "have-nots." I do hope my poem is liked and the message speaks to many.

Just a Gentle Breeze

The wind in Wyoming never stops,
I fell over two years ago, but I still haven't dropped.

It has sucked all the moisture out of my skin,
And now I'm just leather outside and dry bones within.

I have so much darn dirt up my nose,
The Sahara Desert now comes out when it blows.

It can be quite painful when the wind starts to gale,
'Cause I have to hold my hat on with a ten-penny nail.

The water all blows sideways when it rains,
And the bark on the trees is missing out on the plains.

Some days it's just a gentle breeze,
Only moving large rocks and uprooting trees.

Out on the prairie, the horses are all leaning to one side,
And if you're trying to rope,
You'll need to make adjustments as you ride.

You can't throw directly at a critter,
You'll need to use some stealth,
And if you're not careful, you could accidentally rope yourself.

The cows aren't grazing, they're clenching their teeth
With every bite,
Clamping down as best they can, holding on with all their might.

Some days it blows so hard, I can't hear my own words,
Yesterday a conversation from the next county was overheard.

This Wyoming wind always gives us a gentle reminder
That you need to wear steel wool to cover your behind,

Because the other day I decided I'd finally had enough
When the wind ripped off my clothes and left me standing in the buff.

Stacy Jenne
Douglas, WY

Spider on My Windowsill

Life charges on day to day
We humans seem always on our way

So many things call and confuse
He simply builds and waits the muse

He has a castle—it was mine to start
Found in a pet store deco fishing part

Hubby wants him cleaned away
What would friends and neighbors say?

Truly do I really care?
What harm is he doing there?

Keeps me company while I wash and cook
Hope he is always in his little nook!

Barbara Rae Swaniger
Waynesburg, PA

The Puppet

The strings bounded to its arms
They cause no harm
They tell it how to live

The strings can be broken easily
The strings just need a small tug measly
But it is not free

It has no reason to be free
It lives to listen to thee
To be a follower of the strings

The audience sees nothing
The strings aren't something
Just it

When the show starts
It dances
And the show ends
Just the same

All but the puppet
Does not know from where the show has come

Emily Martell
Ashaway, RI

She

She hovers, frayed jeans, hair tousled, a mess of bleach, bronze, and sea,
Quiet as she examines the mismatch of assorted candy.
She's encased within herself, fear gripping and scratching at her,
The clerk, gum smacking, dancing numbers on the register.
She stands, waiting for courage to come, she feels the warmth of sun.
The heat from the Georgia projects warms the rows of the dime store.
A young mother and her boy rustle into the store, faces masked in dirt
    from the city.
They, gathering coins, extracting the lint from the silver, their voices low,
They, commandeering a prize snow cone, bright red hanging smartly in
    its triangle goblet.
She, hands flickering, digging deep in her pockets, hot and sweaty,
Her tongue, lifted gently against the roof of her mouth, pressing back a
    scream.
Her eyes dart, the clerk housed in a blue smock, hair a shade of red not
    found in nature.
She, reaching, grasping, beyond the grip of her morals, the dare still
    stinging in her ears.
She, fingering the Snickers bar, tiny nine-year-old hands, barely able to
    wrap about the bar.
She, turning the bar over, the distance from shelf to pocket, miles apart.
The boy squeals as coins exchange for an icy treat, giddy with relief it promises.
The clerk, tapping fingers, a rhythm, echoing down the rows of Bugles
    and pink Sno Balls,
Rat tat tat, tat tat tat, rat tat tat.
She, grasping the bar tightly, sweat on her brow, throat thick with guilt,
Eyes darting, fear welling deep in her chest, heart pounding in her ears.
The bar, hidden in the folds of her tattered brother's sweater.
The bar, warm in her pocket, heat of her hand, changes shapes in the
    tiny folds of a lie.
She turns, heavy feet, cement made from peers, poured into her shoes.
She walks like a ghost out the door, straight to Sheila, who takes the
    prize and giggles with joy.
The pair, unaware of the dam that's breaking,
For this one act is only the first of many crimes their lives will hold.

Michelle Cruz
South Hadley, MA

Index of Poets

Whitman, Margaret 281
Widner, Sandra 82
Wiles, Lisa 118
Williams, Barbara A. 211
Williams, Chester R. 154
Williams, Joyce 284
Williams, Michelle L. 125
Williams, Stephen R. 55
Wilson, Faith 169
Wilson, Martha E. 278
Winter, Marilyn N. 105
Wishon, Dolores D. 174
Womack, Sarah 184
Wong, Patrick J. 80
Wood, Joan C. 201
Wrobleski, Donna 158

Y

Young, Lena T. 110
Yuzon, Ligaya V. 57

Z

Zink, Steve O. 234